Teaching Recorder in the Music Classroom

Teaching Recorder in the Music Classroom

by Fred Kersten

MENC MENC
MENC MENC The National Association for Music Education

MENC—The National Association for Music Education
1806 Robert Fulton Drive, Reston, VA 20191-4348

Printed in the United States of America.
ISBN: 1-56545-141-4

Dedication

This book is dedicated to Eloise H. Kersten, who has provided motivation, encouragement, and support for the development and continuation of the writing of this manuscript. Thanks, Mom!!

Acknowledgments

The author gratefully acknowledges valuable help from the following individuals:

Ken Andresen, director, Long Island Recorder Orchestra, New York

Donna Basile, elementary school music teacher, Thomas J. Lehey Elementary School, Harborfields, New York

Bob Bergin, president/CEO, Rhythm Band Instruments, Fort Worth, Texas

Brian Blood, managing director (CEO), Dolmetsch Musical Instruments, Surrey, UK

Stan Davis, director, Long Island Recorder Festival, New York

Nickolas Lander, developer of the Recorder Home Page: www.classicolumns.hispeed.com/nickl/recorder.html

Martha Miller, elementary school music teacher, Hollidaysburg Public Schools, Hollidaysburg, Pennsylvania

Eugene Reichenthal, director emeritus, Long Island Recorder Festival, New York

Sue Riley, middle and high school music teacher, South Windsor, Connecticut

Konnie K. Saliba, professor of music education, University of Memphis, Memphis, Tennessee

Contents

Chapter 1

The Recorder in the General Music Classroom

The recorder is one of the most valued resources available to a classroom music teacher. Recorders are inexpensive, widely available, and adaptable to almost any kind of music. Unfortunately, the recorder is sometimes taught by persons with little expertise and knowledge of how to play the instrument, how to locate literature, and how the recorder can and should sound. Taking the time to read this book and familiarizing yourself with this inexpensive, easy-to-learn instrument will bring knowledge and pleasure to you and your students.

Recorder playing is hands-on music education. Players must make musical decisions about tempo, intonation, and balance of parts. In order to achieve success, they must communicate, interact, and cooperate. As each student learns to cover his or her part in the ensemble, opportunities for developing music-reading skills and musical responsibility present themselves. The recorder lends itself to developing competencies within the National Standards guidelines, because recorder playing can complement and be integrated with other classroom activities such as singing, improvisation, composition, and movement.

Recorder playing requires breath control and posture synonymous with proper singing techniques. Indeed, singing and recorder playing can assist each other in helping students to learn sound production skills, pitch awareness, and phrasing.

Recorders appeal to all age-groups. Many individuals continue to play the recorder after their music-class training, and it is not uncommon to find senior citizens who regularly participate in recorder groups and activities. Classroom singing, chorus accompaniment, chamber music, improvisation, and student-created compositions can all involve the recorder ensemble in central or supporting roles. Should you be involved in adult education, continuing education, or church music activities, you will find that recorder ensembles are an excellent medium for exploring musical concepts and developing music appreciation, as well as providing opportunities for public performance.

What will you and your students gain directly from recorder ensemble activities? Instead of playing unison melody on soprano recorders with obvious intonation differences, students can discover multipart harmony through ensemble experiences. They can learn to take responsibility for part playing while experiencing ensemble literature, and you can teach music reading, repertoire, intonation awareness, and appreciation skills without excessive expense for instruments and music.

This book focuses on practical ideas that may be used in K–12 classrooms. It is based on the experience of the author, a veteran public school music teacher, and on input from many individuals who teach recorder playing in public school classes. No one method or approach has been intentionally emphasized over others; however, the Orff Schulwerk approach receives attention because of its extensive utilization of the recorder. The information presented here is an attempt to improve recorder playing of students at all levels.

The recorder is sometimes made more challenging to learn than it needs to be because of a lack of information that hinders teachers who want to demonstrate its qualities and idiosyncracies accurately and effectively to their students. Unfortunately, the recorder is sometimes perceived as a toy because many models are made of plastic and because an inferior quality of playing sometimes results from poor teaching methods. It is also seen as a child-oriented, preband instrument, equated with classroom rhythm instruments. The public has little awareness of its history, artistry, and musical potential. Sadly, within the secondary school curriculum, when the recorder's value for ensemble possibilities is at its greatest, it is not featured as strongly as it could be. A multitude of creative opportunities exists for musical development of students in upper-level general music classes at a time in their lives when they are often seeking opportunities for individual and group expression. This "underdog" of instruments can provide new opportunities for musical activities and performance.

I have tried to include information of interest to players at all levels of proficiency. This information is provided with the suggestion that you as a teacher adopt this instrument as a vehicle for your own musicanship. Teachers perform on all varieties of orchestral, band, and keyboard instruments—why don't they consider the recorder as an interesting solo instrument? There is extensive high-quality solo and ensemble literature that can grace recitals, assemblies, and community performances. The recorder can readily furnish your students with a means of performing and provide you with a medium for further developing your own musicality and musicianship.

As more and more contemporary composers create literature for it, the recorder is being rediscovered and is regaining popularity. It is effective as a solo instrument when used with contrasting timbre accompaniments such as guitar, strings, or the multitude of timbres available from a classroom electronic keyboard or synthesizer. It is a great foil for the rhythms and timbres of a percussion ensemble or rhythm band.

For many who have not experienced the cohesive sound, personal satisfaction, and musicality of group instrumental performance, recorder playing provides a very musical opportunity for participation, especially at the junior- and senior-high school level. Students not involved in the traditional band, orchestra, and choral ensembles can benefit, because they can participate in performance opportunities even if they have not previously been involved in a school music program.

A recorder orchestra is fulfilling and fun, and the lower-range instruments can provide balance to the brilliant and sometimes shrill characteristics of alto and soprano recorders. Orchestral transcriptions making use of the full range of pitches have been arranged from works by composers such as Bach, Mozart, and Mussorgsky. Contemporary compositions are being written specifically for the recorder ensemble's tonal resources and the idiomatic characteristics of the instrument. Many recorder festivals, such as the annual Gene Reichenthal Day Recorder Festival held on Long Island in New York, provide opportunities for group playing.

It is possible to begin teaching a recorder class using only this book and a limited amount of sheet music. But each program is unique, and a teacher who is interested in developing his or her own program needs access to plenty of resources. Detailed, comprehensive information is available in Chapter 9, Literature and Other Resources, which also provides details for the resources recommended in Chapters 1–8.

Chapter 2

Introducing the Recorder

This chapter provides an overview of the history of the recorder, a brief description of its design, and a few interesting facts about the instrument that can be shared with students. No attempt has been made to provide a comprehensive body of detailed information, which is readily available in many of the resources suggested in Chapter 9.

The History and Development of the Recorder

Based on the discovery of a Neanderthal flute made from the femur bone of a bear cub, the use of early instrumental ancestors of the recorder is estimated to have begun between 43,000 and 82,000 years ago. This flute was found in Slovenia by Kvan Turk of the Slovenian Academy of Paleontology.[1] A recorder can be seen in a fourteenth-century fresco (*The Mocking of Jesus,* 1315 A.D.) located in the Church of Staro Nagoricvino, near Kumanova in Macedonia. In this fresco, a musician plays a cylindrical duct flute, the window/labium of which is clearly visible. (The term "duct" [from the Latin "ductus," meaning "windway"] refers to the space between the block and the top of the beak that allows the air to enter the recorder and be focused on the lip or labium.) At the foot of the instrument in the fresco, there is an open finger hole for the little finger of the lowermost hand.[2]

A fourteenth-century recorder, a two-piece instrument with holes for seven fingers and a thumb, was found in northern Germany in 1987. Full consorts of recorders (SATB) were produced in the fifteenth through sixteenth centuries. They had conical bores, full rich tone, and a range of one octave and a sixth. Redesigned solo recorders appeared in the late 1600s. These three-piece Baroque recorders were capable of playing a chromatic scale of two and one-half octaves and had a strong reedy tone.

The recorder was part of the musical life in the American colonies, and many early settlers played this instrument. The first known band identified in America was formed in 1653 and included recorders, which were considerably quieter than the other instruments, such as the two drums and fifteen oboes, that also comprised the group.[3]

During the Classical and Romantic periods, the recorder was used very little as the emphasis was on orchestral instruments with extensive note ranges and a multitude of dynamic possibilities. Recorders were used, however, to provide marching music during the Civil War.[4]

Interest in the recorder returned in Europe at the turn of the twentieth century with the rediscovery of early music. The early twentieth-century American revival of the recorder was spurred by performances of Arnold Dolmetsch in Europe and the Trapp Family Singers. Interest developed further through the activities of the American Recorder Society, which was founded in 1939.

The Design of the Recorder

Recorders have been made of materials including plexiglass, ivory, bone, porcelain, glass, metals, and even cement. Wood recorders are made from maple, boxwood, rosewood, ebony, and other soft and hard woods. Harder woods are more impervious to moisture and hold heat longer, allowing for stability of intonation.

Sound is produced as the air stream hits the lip. Approximately half of the air goes out of the recorder through the lip opening, and the rest goes into the instrument, escaping through the holes and bell. The quality of the sound is determined by a waveform that is developed as the air is divided by the lip. If an equal division is made, the wave is more like a pure sine wave. Unequal divisions produce a more "reedy" tone.

Recorders have sometimes been called "fipple flutes" because of the "fipple" or block located inside wooden recorders. (Some plastic ones have removable blocks, but they are usually built in.) A fipple is a small, removable block of cedar that is placed in the head joint of the instrument. It forms the floor of the windway and connects through to the window, which allows the concentration of air on the lip to produce the recorder's whistle-like sound.

Twentieth-century redesigns to improve the recorder include the production of ABS plastic recorders. Instruments are also made of both plastic and wood, with the head portion of the instrument made of plastic while the body is made of wood.

A square recorder was developed in 1975 by Joachim and Herbert Paetzold in Germany. These instruments resemble a square organ pipe and are made of plywood, thus reducing instrument cost. Although uncommon, some recorders have add-ons such as "piano/forte" keys to play soft or loud and/or a "bell key" to cover the bell aperture for improving upper-tone production. In recent years, recorders intended for use with individuals who are physically challenged have been developed. These recorders can be adjusted to meet specific finger and hand requirements. Pentatonic recorders (which allow only the notes of the pentatonic scale to be played) are also available for classroom use.

Twenty-first century recorder designs include the Mollenhauer Modern Alto, which increases the length of the recorder, adding a third octave of pitches and an increased level of volume. New acoustic designs include self-contained microphones that amplify sound. Electronic wind controllers are also available. These breath-regulated devices control synthesizers that can reproduce the sound of the recorder and other timbres.

Interesting Facts about the Recorder

Why the instrument is named the "recorder" is not known. Some European-language names for the recorder, which are based on characteristics of its sound and the head joint, are *flauto dolce* (Italian for "sweet-sounding flute"), *blockflöte* (German for "fipple flute"), *flute à bec* (French for "beak flute").

Recorders range in size from the subcontrabass recorder in the key of C to the garklein, which is pitched in C and is the smallest recorder readily available. The piccolino recorder, which is pitched in F-minor and made by Frans van Twaalfhoven of the Netherlands, has a range of one octave above the sopranino recorder, making the piccolino the highest pitched recorder. The piccolino is played by interleaving the digits of each hand, although the fingering sequence remains the same.[5]

Many players use a vibrato that can be produced using the diaphragm, throat, or the fingers. "Flattement" is a type of vibrato produced by using the fingers to produce a pitch fluctuation by slightly covering and uncovering a hole to slightly change the pitch. (As the word implies, the sound is usually flatter than the original note played.) The vibrato rate may be made slower or faster at the discretion of the player.

The recorder has a conical bore that is different from other instruments in that it is larger at the top and smaller at the bottom. The pipe organ, sometimes called the "king of instruments," consists of hundreds and thousands of pipes that are of construction similar to the recorder. The organ's flue pipes (flutes and principals) are most similar to the recorder because each has a lip and a windway. Playing one recorder sound on the pipe organ uses approximately sixty-one flue pipes.

To warm their recorders before playing a recital and to keep them warm between pieces, some professional recorder players cover their instruments with hot water bottles or electric blankets.

A study by Lorretto conducted in 1993 estimates that over three and a half million recorders are manufactured each year.[6]

Notes

1. Robert Fink, "Neanderthal Flute: Oldest Music Instrument's Four Notes Match Four of Do, Re, Mi Scale," (1997), From the Musicological Analysis Web site: www.webster.sk.ca/greenwich/fl-compl.htm.

2. N. S. Lander, "The Recorder: Instrument of Torture or Instrument of Music?" (1996–1999), from the Recorder Home Page: members.iinet.net.au/~nickl/torture2.html.

3. Clifford Bevan, et al.,"Band," in *New Grove Dictionary of Musical Instruments,* ed. Stanley Sadie (London: Macmillan Press, 1984), Volume 1:120–43.

4. D. Waitzman, "The Decline of the Recorder in the 18th Century," *Recorder & Music Magazine* 2, no. 7 (1967): 222–25.

5. N. S. Lander, "Extant Recorder Makers & Retailers" (1996–99), from the Recorder Home Page: members.iinet.net.au/~nickl/makers.html #Twaalfhovern.

6. A. Loretto, "Plastic Recorders," *Recorder and Music* 13, no. 1 (1993): 3–4, 8.

Chapter 3

Selecting and Purchasing Recorders

Obtaining thirty or more recorders for a general music class requires some forethought. This chapter addresses how to plan the purchases. It also includes discussions about the pros and cons of wood vs. plastic, the ranges and types of recorders, and how to accommodate physically challenged students so that they can play the recorder successfully. While this information is important for decision-making, there is nothing like holding an actual recorder and making music with it to help one decide whether or not to purchase it. See the Try It Yourself sidebar for what to look for when you are evaluating recorders to purchase for your students.

Planning the Purchase

There are many approaches to acquiring recorders. Students may purchase their own soprano instruments, or if your budget permits, you can purchase new ones for children entering grade three, thereby ensuring that a recorder will be provided for each child throughout the years he or she participates in your music classes.

Another approach to providing recorders for beginning students is to purchase enough instruments for one class (about thirty) and sterilize them each time they are used. Sterilization dips are available at approximately $7.50 a gallon, or you can use a more convenient spray bottle. These products, which are used for other band and orchestra wind instruments, can be obtained through most music supply stores. Students' involvement in this disinfecting of their instruments helps to develop their awareness of hygiene, as the instruments must be sprayed or dipped

Try It Yourself

The best procedure to ensure compatible intonation and tone is to obtain an "on-approval recorder" and try it yourself. Test the instrument for accurate intonation (obtain a tuner from your band director) and check different notes. When the head joint is pushed all the way in, which pitch do you get? A-440, lower, or higher? Or, do you have to pull out the head joint to get this approximate pitch? Does it play "stuffy"? (As if something is stuck in the instrument that causes resistance and/or prevents playing a full, direct tone.) Does it clog easily? How hard do you have to blow to get an accurate sound? If the instrument does not play well for you, your students will most likely have problems too.

in a container of solution prior to each class. The advantages of purchasing a smaller number of higher quality instruments are that they are better in tune and cost less than purchasing individual instruments for each student in the school. Disadvantages include children being unable to take the instruments home to practice and the inconvenience of frequent dipping or spraying.

To provide ensemble opportunities for your students, you can request that the larger tenor and bass recorders be purchased by the school. Financing these more expensive instruments may be a problem; however, the expenditure will give you the opportunity to create numerous ensembles and teach an unlimited number of students in the future.

An optimum number of bass and tenor instruments that would give flexibility and opportunity for a variety of recorder ensemble activities would include four bass recorders at approximately $250 per instrument and four tenors at approximately $60 each, for a total expenditure of about $1,240, which may not be approved as a lump sum budget item. However, if you increase your recorder inventory by one instrument each year (start with one bass and one tenor recorder) and can show results, your small annual requisitions may be approved (develop a log of use, and be sure to identify students who did not previously participate in other school-sponsored performance ensembles).

Contrabass recorders, which are constructed out of plywood and are becoming more common, are desirable but expensive. However, a synthesizer flute patch can be used quite effectively for the bottom voices, and these instruments are common in most schools. With these instruments as a nucleus, the formation of a recorder orchestra, a bass recorder ensemble, and various SATB groups is possible, not only for the students, but for a continuing-education community ensemble. (If you develop a community ensemble, soprano, alto, and sopranino recorders could be provided by members, and the cost of purchasing these instruments would be eliminated.)

What to Buy

When purchasing recorders, try to identify one specific make or model that you prefer and purchase it consistently. Intonation difficulties are minimized when all instruments are made by the same manufacturer. Specify soprano recorders with Baroque (English) fingering, not German fingering. Buy instruments with double holes, not single ones. German fingering does simplify the fingering required of the right hand to play the note F; the index, ring, and pinky fingers do not have to cover holes simultaneously. Yet, while this may offer a slight advantage initially, German instruments have many intonation difficulties, and there is a later transfer-of-learning problem, because other recorders in the family do not use this system.

Some teachers endorse one- or two-piece recorders to reduce problems that can occur when the foot-joints of three-piece recorders move out of line or come off. However, other teachers prefer three-piece recorders because the holes on the foot joint can be adjusted to each student's hand. Have each student find the best section alignment that provides maximum hole covering and optimum finger comfort. To make sure that the pieces of a recorder stay in line, take some liquid page correction fluid and paint it over the section joints, especially the small foot joint. Then draw a line across the joint on the dry fluid using a pen or magic marker. If the section is turned out of position or comes off, simply have the player realign the two marks, and the recorder will be back in order

Thumb Rests

Thumb rests can be of help in establishing good hand position and developing support. Slip-on thumb rests are preferable to those molded in position because hand sizes vary, and the fixed position thumb rest may place the right hand in an uncomfortable or awkward position. When you find an optimum position for the slip-on thumb rest, use the correction fluid method to draw lines so that proper position may be quickly restored if the rest is moved.

Lanyards

Some recorders are available with an attached lanyard that can be placed over the neck. If students are involved in activities that require frequent alternating of playing, moving, and clapping activities, recorders with lanyards can be helpful because they are always at hand, not on the floor or a desk. Lanyards also offer a resting position for the recorder during times that students are not called upon to play.

Bass Pegs

When you purchase a bass recorder (approximately $250), you should also buy a bass peg, which allows the bass recorder to be played without the neck strap. It is similar to the peg found on a bass clarinet or cello and costs about $35. The bass peg, which attaches with velcro that is included, eliminates the need for a neck strap and makes holding the bass recorder easy.

Plastic or Wood?

Many quality recorders made of ABS plastic are fully compatible with their wooden peers. New directions in production have improved plastic instruments, which in many cases are modeled after original instruments that are famous for their quality sound and intonation. Molded plastic instruments can have a high degree of reliability in their ability to replicate the qualities and intonation of their prototypes. This does not mean, however, that they are perfectly in tune with themselves or with other recorders, as there are variations between manufacturers. To minimize irregularities, it is strongly suggested that you use one brand and model for all your classes. This way, all the instruments will be in tune or out of tune together.

You may purchase recorders that contain both plastic and wood components. The head joint (also called the fipple or whistle) is made of plastic, and the body is made of wood. Maintenance is simple. Because it is plastic, the head joint can be cleaned with soap and water, while the body provides the tonal advantages of wood. These newer models also are lower in cost than models made entirely out of wood. As your students progress, you may wish to feature these instruments as higher-end solo recorders or as the next step up from generic classroom instruments.

Recorders with Pentatonic Scales

Several makers build recorders that produce pentatonic scales. Essentially, these instruments play just the notes of a pentatonic scale and can be used with Orff or Kodály teaching strategies. These instruments are ideal for improvisation activities over fixed borduns and can also be used in playing many folk tunes that are pentatonic-based. Pentatonic recorders are available in soprano, alto, and tenor, and some one-piece instruments in the keys of C, F, G, and D come with four or five holes. Kelischek Workshop is one source of plastic models (see Chapter 9).

You do not need a large quantity of these instruments. Several can be effectively used to enhance your singing activities and provide a variety of lessons. For example, if you use the soprano pentatonic recorder in C, your students can freely improvise initially without concern about the correctness of notes, because any of the tones will work. This is a great option for reducing the inhibitions of beginners who might not feel comfortable trying to improvise.

Tonal Ranges

Recorders come in six tonal ranges: sopranino, soprano, alto, tenor, bass, and contrabass. A brief description of the costs and uses of each follows.

Soprano recorders come at varying prices. You can obtain one for as little as two dollars from some vendors, and prices range upwards to $15 for top-of-the-line plastics. Wood instruments range from $40 to $400, depending on the make of the recorder and the type of wood used. Many lower-priced instruments have intonation problems, as well as tonal qualities and blowing resistance that can limit and inhibit beginning students. Plastic recorders sometimes come with a book or are packaged with a CD or an audio cassette. You may save on such packages, but you may also be obliged to sacrifice in terms of instrumental and instructional quality. Regardless of the bargains that abound, it is wise to consider purchasing the best plastic recorder you can afford. Because of the expense, you may have to purchase fewer instruments: however, the ones you have will be better quality instruments.

Consider making good quality ***alto instruments*** available to fifth- and six-grade students who have mastered the soprano recorder and need a challenge. Purchase several alto recorders and use the disinfectant method of sterilizing them. The cost of plastic alto recorders ranges from $15 to $60. If you purchase ten alto recorders each year, within three years you will have enough instruments for your upper grade classes. For the first year, you can immediately start teaching if you rotate instruments among members of your class (disinfecting the mouthpieces, as discussed earlier), having one-third play alto recorder while the other two-thirds play soprano recorders. Since the majority of the serious solo literature is written for alto recorder, these instruments are important to include in the classroom budget because they will continue to be useful at the secondary level through grade twelve.

A plastic ***tenor recorder*** (obtain one with both low C and C# keys) costs approximately $75. Aulos produces a plastic tenor recorder that has holes that are closer together than those of standard recorders, reducing the stretch for individuals with small hands or a smaller finger spread. Newer designs include the "knick tenor," an instrument with a mitered neck that allows players with limited reach to play with more comfort.

The ***sopranino recorder*** is pitched an octave above the alto recorder. It is valuable for playing descants and obbligatos, doubling melody parts for brilliance, and enhancing singing activities. At a cost of $10–15, it is well worth the investment because students are attracted to its bright, sparkling tone color and its small size.

Plastic ***bass recorders*** are available with "knick" necks (mitered necks); with direct air stream mouthpieces (a person blows directly into the cap of the recorder); or with a "bocal," a metal tube like that on a bassoon that connects into the top of the recorder cap and extends downward. The mitered bass recorder allows easier hand reach and usually requires a neck strap, and it is easier for persons of small stature to play. Consider purchasing this type of bass recorder (approximately $250) and a bass peg for it.

The ***contrabass recorder*** is pitched one octave below the bass recorder. Because of its cost (approximately two to eight thousand dollars), it is rarely found in school or community ensembles. Currently however, this instrument is becoming more available because the use of plywood instead of more expensive hardwoods and square instead of round construction have lowered cost. Should it be available, this instrument provides an excellent foundation for any recorder ensemble. Substituting the recorder or flute patch on a synthesizer is a possibility and is encouraged to balance the sometimes overly treble nature of recorder ensembles with the lower tones of the contrabass.

Physically Challenged Students

Physically challenged students can benefit from instruments made by Dolmetsch and Aulos that are designed to accommodate hands with limited flexibility, short fingers, or missing digits. Players can adjust removable sections to positions that make it easier for them to produce a sound or accommodate a hand with a missing digit. Once a recorder has been customized, it can be glued to set its sections permanently in position.

Dolmetsch Gold series recorders are designed with four keys, to compensate for a missing finger or thumb, and they incorporate a two-position thumb key (closed/open), operated via a key with the smallest finger of the usable hand. The Gold series recorders are made of wood and are custom-designed with gold keys. (Gold is used because some individuals may have allergies to nickel.) Wood choices include pearwood, boxwood, or rosewood, and the recorder can be adapted for either the left or right hand. Alto and soprano recorders are available.

The Aulos 204AF recorder allows the player to adjust a moveable section to a hole position that makes it easier to produce a

Figure 1
Aulos 204AF recorder with moveable sections

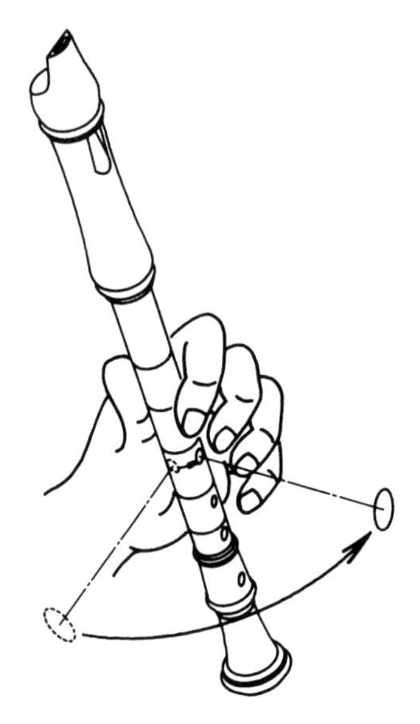

Source: Reprinted with permission from Toyama. ©2000 by Toyama. Not for further reproduction without express written permission from Toyama.

Figure 2
Separable parts of the Aulos 204AF recorder

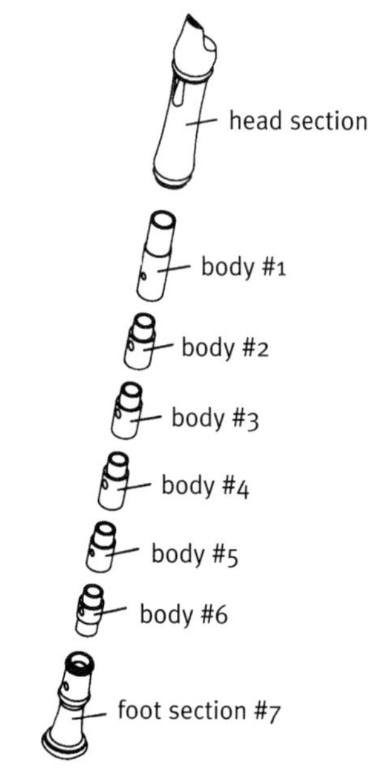

Source: Reprinted with permission from Toyama. ©2000 by Toyama. Not for further reproduction without express written permission from Toyama.

sound, or to accommodate a hand with a missing digit. (See Figure 1, Aulos 204AF Recorder with Moveable Sections). Once the recorder has been customized, it can be glued to permanently keep the sections in place. A total of six sections plus head and foot sections can be connected and rotated. (See Figure 2, Separable Parts of the Aulos 204AF Recorder.) In certain circumstances, the holes may be plugged. Individuals with short fingers, paralysis, arthritis, or missing fingers can play a chromatic scale as long as six fingers are functional. The Aulos 204AF recorder is available from Rhythm Band Instruments.

Marsha Evans has written about using the recorder with physically challenged students.[1] Figure 3, Fingering Charts for Six, Seven,

Figure 3

Fingering charts for six, seven, and eight fingers

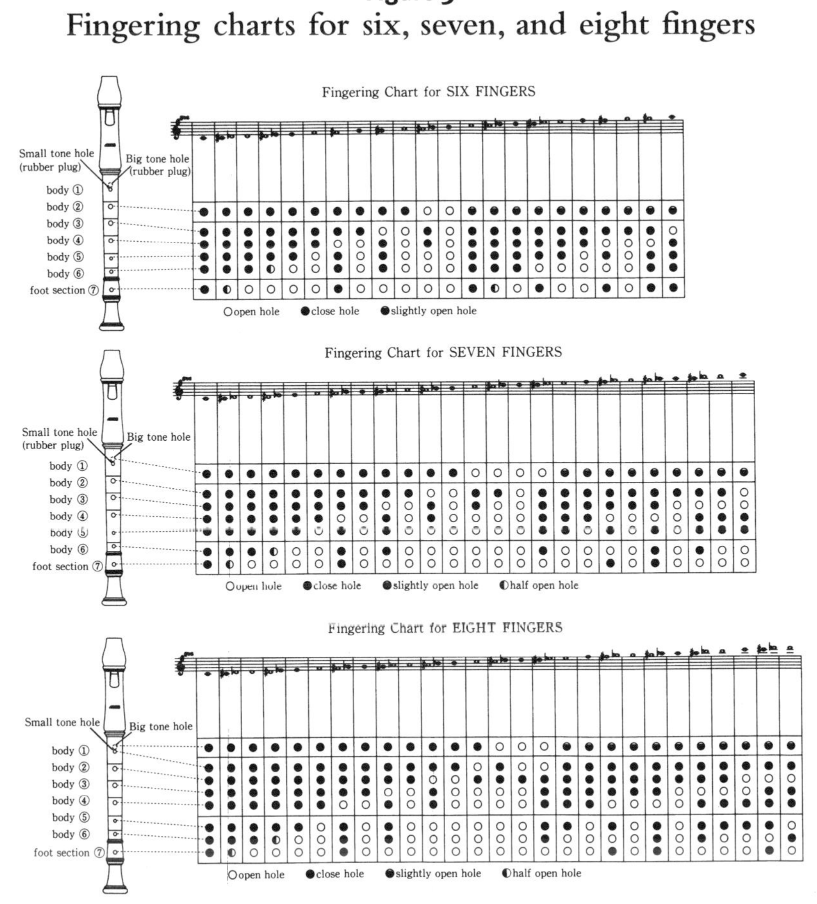

Source: Reprinted with permission from Toyama. ©2000 by Toyama. Not for further reproduction without express written permission from Toyama.

and Eight Fingers, can help individuals who do not have full use of all their fingers. (Standard fingering charts are in the appendix.)

Note

1. Marsha Evans, "New Aulos Recorder for Disabled Opens Door to Music for Many," *The American Recorder* 3, no. 5 (November 1993): 3.

Chapter 4

Recorder Basics

To be successful, an aspiring recorder player needs to do more than pick up an instrument, learn a few fingerings, and start blowing notes. As with other wind instruments, playing the recorder requires correct body, hand, wrist, and finger positions. To optimize tone production, the player must also have good embouchure and know how to breathe and tongue properly. And, although the recorder's construction may be simple and the instrument relatively inexpensive, it needs proper cleaning and maintenance. This chapter addresses these basic essentials.

Body Position

Good posture and relaxed muscles are vital to obtaining a quality sound from the recorder, but it cannot be assumed that students know how to do these things "naturally." Full, sonorous, unstrained sound can result only if the body is optimally aligned for breathing out sustained and controlled air. Both standing and sitting positions should be taught. This is especially important for classroom teachers whose students sit at their desks or on the floor in circles. Whether students stand or sit, their shoulders should be relaxed, and their elbows should be parallel to their rib cages. (Holding the arms up and away from the body produces tension that diminishes the quality of the sound that is produced.)

Alternating singing and recorder playing can be a beneficial practice in the music classroom. Diaphragm control, physical relaxation, open throat, accurate articulation, and proper breathing are synonymous with correct, effective singing as well as recorder playing. Each activity can effectively and efficiently reinforce the other.

Figure 1
Hand position diagram

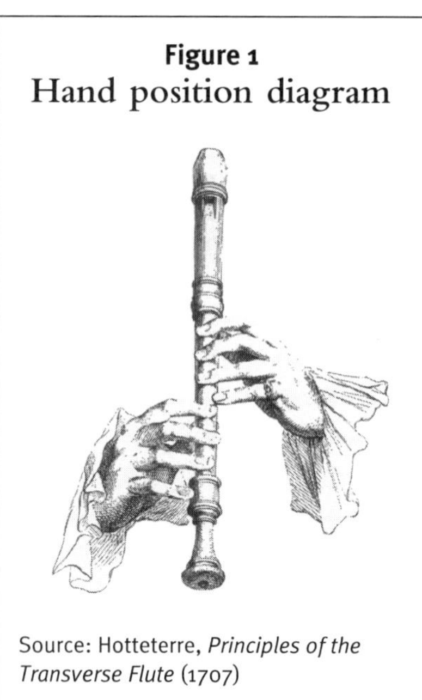

Source: Hotteterre, *Principles of the Transverse Flute* (1707)

Hand Position

Incorrect hand position results in tense hands and partially covered holes, which are the causes of many problems related to low-note production. The right-hand fingers should be placed at approximately a right angle to the holes. It is allowable for the fingers to extend a little over the side of the recorder (see Figure 1, Hand Position Diagram). In this position, the pad of the finger is over the hole. Finger numbers on the recorder are as follows:

- ***Left Hand.*** Thumb: T; Index: 1; Middle: 2; Ring: 3; (the left-hand pinky is not used, or it is sometimes rests on the recorder and stabilizes the instrument.)

- ***Right Hand.*** Index: 4; Middle: 5; Ring: 6; Pinky: 7.

Finger numbering diagram

① L.H. 1st
② L.H. 2nd
③ L.H. 3rd
④ R.H. 1st
⑤ R.H. 2nd
⑥ R.H. 3rd
⑦ R.H. 4th
L. Thumb
R. Thumb (for balance)

- the left hand should always be at the top of the recorder.
- The first three holes and the thumb hole are covered with the left hand fingers.
- The right thumb is used to balance the recorder
- Holes 4, 5, 6, and 7 are covered with the right hand fingers.

Source: *Hands On Recorder*, Book One in Sweet Pipes Recorder Series. Ft. Worth, TX: Sweet Pipes, 1995), p. 3. Used by permission.

Maintaining the exact finger position is not as critical to good playing as maintaining a relaxed hand position is. It is important to keep the hands relaxed, almost to the point that the instrument falls out of the fingers. Support for the recorder should come from the right thumb, the little finger of the right hand, and the lips. Tell your students to keep the left thumb relaxed as it is constantly moving and should not be used for support.

Right-Hand Pinky Position

Eugene Reichenthal, a noted and experienced teacher of recorder to children, recommends utilizing the right-hand little finger to help balance the instrument.[1] The right-hand pinky is placed on the recorder, near and to the right of the lowest hole. It moves only to cover the hole to play C or C#. This position is easy to teach, and it provides another location for recorder support in addition to the thumb and lip.

Left-Hand Thumb Pinch or Roll

The thumb on the left hand is involved in almost every note the recorder plays, and there are many opinions about how it should function. Many players "roll" the thumb away from the hole or "pinch" it back at the first joint to expose a half-hole to change registers or to play other notes.

A good way to explain thumb movement to your students is to tell them to bend the thumb at the first joint slightly, which rolls the left corner of the thumb away from the hole. This modified pinch requires minimal movement and provides a degree of precision and accuracy in opening the same amount of aperture each time. For most notes, a hole shaped like a crescent moon will suffice; however, for certain upper notes, this space may be increased towards a half-moon shape to improve intonation. Each player should be encouraged to experiment to find the best position for himself or herself.

Remind your students about the importance of keeping the left thumb nail trimmed and filed. A ragged nail can damage the thumb hole, and any space between the nail and flesh can allow air to leak out when the student's fingers are on the holes, adversely affecting note production.

Playing Double Holes—Right-Hand Wrist Rotation

Recorders with double holes, which provide a more accurate way of playing chromatic lower tones, are preferred over those with single holes. Use the wrist as a pivot to improve control and accuracy so that the same amount of the right-hand pinky and ring finger is moved on and off the hole each time the notes are played.

Common Articulations

Articulation	Use
tu, ti, ta	strong normal tonguing
du, di, da	weaker normal tonguing
dit	staccato
ru, na	legato tonguing
did-dle	double tonguing
tu-ku-tu	triple tonguing

To show your students how to do this, place both hands on the recorder with fingers T, 1, 2, 3, 4, 5, 6, and 7 covering the holes and the right-hand thumb in its support position under the recorder. As you pull your little finger away from the back double-hole C on the soprano recorder to play C-sharp, rotate your right wrist towards your upper body at the point of the raised wrist bone. You are sliding the little finger away from the C hole. Then slide the little finger back using the wrist as a fulcrum, rotating in the other direction to play C. Try the same thing with D and D sharp using the ring finger. Have your students repeat your motions on their own recorders. With a little bit of practice, each student will learn how much of his or her wrist to move to obtain a precise sound. Emphasizing a "slide" feeling will reduce pressure on the fingers and improve legato and speed. When they can slide their fingers across comfortably to play C, D, and D-sharp, add various articulations like "du," "tu," and "ru" and coordinate each with a change in the note. Practicing these motions should help students to eliminate "blurps" and "blops" between tones. See the Common Articulations sidebar for a list of articulations and their uses.

Correct Embouchure

As with playing other wind instruments, having a correct embouchure helps to play the recorder well. Familiarize yourself with the recorder's embouchure before you demonstrate it to

Figure 2
Diagram of instrument parts

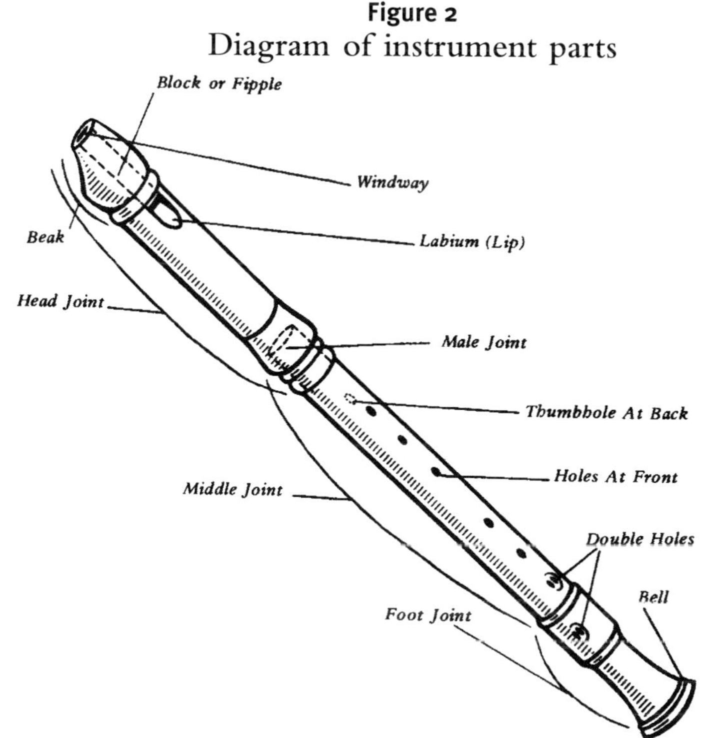

Source: *The Recorder Player's Handbook*, by Hans-Martin Linde. James C. Haden, trans. (Miami, Florida: Warner Bros., 1974). Used by permission.

your students. Put the recorder between your lips as if forming a kiss. The angle of the recorder should be between thirty and eighty degrees away from the chin and slightly to the right (approximately ten to twenty degrees to the right) with the teeth slightly parted so the air flow is direct into the windway of the head joint (see Figure 2, Diagram of Instrument Parts). Unlike clarinet playing, the chin is not pointed. Check for air leakage around the beak, especially where the lips join together.

Many students constrict their throats without realizing it when they attempt to blow into the recorder. Sometimes, by singing into the instrument, a player can learn to recognize how the throat should feel when it is relaxed and open. Teach your students to think, "Whistle!" just before they begin to blow. Tell them to position the instrument approximately four to six inches away from the lips, form the lips as if to whistle, and then blow a strong, focused, steady stream of air toward the aperture to produce a sound. As they put their lips around the beak, have your students try to continue this "whistle" feeling. This exercise also aids in learning the concepts of focus and steady air flow.

Correcting Poor Hand Position

Learning good hand and finger position while simultaneously learning blowing and tonguing can be a bit overwhelming, especially for younger students. If students can temporarily put aside learning the multifaceted aspects of blowing and tonguing, they can concentrate on working specifically to improve their hand and finger positions. Here are a few ideas for helping students to improve their hand positions.

Make a paper recorder "master" with recorder holes printed on it and hand out copies to students. Allow your students to customize their paper recorders using magic markers, stick-on stars, circular pieces of cardboard, or other paste-ons to aid tactile location of the holes. (Print extras as sometimes these instruments "break.") Have them roll up and tape the seam to form the paper into a cylinder. Tell them to hold the paper instrument gently so as not to alter the cylindrical shape.

Have them place one end of the cylinder on their chins and "play" the notes, allowing their fingers to move close to the paper with little upward motion, as they chant the melody in syllables or chant the rhythm. Then have them "play" their paper recorders again, this time singing the melody. Make sure that they place their fingers straight across the holes. (Keeping the fingers straight but not tense helps those with smaller hands to extend their reach.)

When playing their actual recorders, the students can learn to assess their pressure and finger-locations by looking at the impressions left on their fingers after they cover the holes. If there is a slight circle on the finger, then it is well placed. You must be careful about how you address this issue with your students. Too much finger pressure produces stiff fingers and tension in the hand. Warn them that pressing as hard as possible to obtain an impression is not the goal. Emphasize that they should use just enough pressure to cover the holes. When the hole is covered, very little additional pressure is needed.

Detachable Thumb Rests

There are many opinions both for and against the use of thumb rests. They can be of help in establishing good hand position and developing support, but they can also be a hindrance if they are improperly placed. A badly positioned thumb rest can cause tension in the right hand and thus restrict movement or accelerate playing fatigue. On some instruments, thumb rests molded in position may be an impediment because hand sizes vary. Using a permanently fixed thumb rest as a guide may immediately place the right hand in an uncomfortable, out-of-line position. These problems can be circumvented with the slip-on thumb rests that are available. If you decide to use a thumb rest, find an optimal position for the slip-on thumb rest and use correction fluid to draw lines so that the proper position may be quickly restored if the thumb rest is moved. If it slides out of position too easily, place a small piece of tape on the concave inner surface of the rest to provide a snugger fit.

To find the best position for your thumb, hold the recorder horizontally with the right hand only, balancing it with the first finger (4), pinky (7), and your right thumb. The thumb should naturally fall to the balance point of the fulcrum. Many players place the thumb rest a little higher than the balance point to prevent the instrument from slipping and to serve as a guide for locating the correct hand position quickly. Placing the thumb rest at a higher position provides a guide for location and support while allowing freedom of movement.

Some recorder teachers feel that, if the recorder is held at a steeper vertical angle (more like a trumpet), the thumb can provide better support, and the recorder can be balanced with less risk of it slipping from the player's hand. In this case, the thumb rest can be eliminated, as the lips, right-hand thumb, and right-hand little finger can support the instrument.

Tonguing

Before you introduce tonguing to students, have them practice speaking the articulation syllables of a simple song. Tell them to place the beaks of their recorders on their chins and then articulate-chant or articulate-sing the passage using Ts and Ds. Not only does this exercise develop awareness of articulation, but it is also useful for exploring phrasing and breathing. Then move slowly into tonguing (using syllables such as "ru" or "na" for slurrings and legato passages), ensuring that your students can do soft tonguing before you introduce them to double and triple tonguing.

Pronunciation for Good Articulation

The sides of the tongue should rest lightly on the top teeth, and the tip of the tongue should touch the palate just above the front teeth. Some teachers feel that the mouth aids in the instrument's resonance and that the player should think of having an apple in his or her mouth, but this approach places the tongue at the bottom of the mouth. The tongue then has a greater distance to travel to reach the palate, which slows tonguing. The important thing is to produce a strong, focused air flow as if whistling. Aim the air so it flows down the front teeth and is focused out just under the top lip.

Various combinations of consonants and vowels are used in tonguing. "T" and "d" are used to produce stronger and weaker attacks. "Ru" is helpful for legato, as is "na." "T" and "d" can be combined with the vowels "a," "e," "i," "o," and "u." "Dit" works well for staccato. "Tu" and "du" can be used for marcato and legato passages. Some players believe that using the syllables "ti" and "di" raise the back of the tongue so that the air flow is more directed.

To end a note, put a "d" on the vowel ("tu—d") or, for a more natural ending to the sound, inhale the air back into the instrument. Many instrumentalists say an unvoiced "huh" as they inhale the air back, thus ending the sound. This technique eliminates the chronic flatting and decreasing dynamics that can sometimes occur when the pitch and sound "dribble off."

Soft Tonguing

Soft tonguing is easy to learn. It basically uses a nonplosive, such as "ru" or "na," which aids in the initial starting of the sound and results in an unarticulated attack. It is also important in slurred and legato passages. Once soft tonguing is mastered, legato playing improves quickly. Example 1 should be articulated as "du-ru" or "tu-ru," depending on the strength desired for the first articulated note.

Example 1

An exercise for soft tonguing

As shown in Example 2, a legato passage might be tongued "du, ru, ru ru, ru, ru, du."

Example 2

An exercise for legato playing

Double and Triple Tonguing

Double and triple tonguing allows the recorder player to produce multiple movements of the tongue, resulting in faster articulation with less effort. The process involves using different syllable combinations to make the tongue provide additional articulations. Syllables such as "did-dle" might be used for double tonguing and "tu-ku-tu" for triple tonguing, instead of the single-tongued "tu."

Knowing how to do double tonguing is very important for recorder players. As students become more advanced, double tonguing provides a challenge and eventually an advantage because eighth- and sixteenth-note passages can be rapidly articulated with half the work that single tonguing requires. As a player becomes proficient and wishes to play many of the quality works available for recorder, double- and triple-tonguing are important techniques to master. Let your students say the articulations first and then try them on single notes. "Did-dle" and "tu-ku-tu" (see Example 3) are good articulations to employ.

Example 3
An exercise for double and triple tonguing

A goal to work toward is double tonguing a C-scale up and down on soprano recorder using "did-dle" for articulation. Slow playing is necessary to achieve coordination (see Example 4).

Example 4
An exercise for double tonguing

Once your students have developed coordination, have them work for speed. Apply the same process to learning triple-tonguing, except have students triple-tongue up and down the scale with one complete articulation on each note.

Breathing

Proper breathing ensures solid, well-formed notes that are pleasing to the ear. Most people underblow, perceiving the instrument's sound as delicate, and all they produce are anemic, out-of-tune tones. The recorder is merely a tube that very accurately reflects the air blown into it and, more specifically, how that air is blown. Of all woodwind instruments, the recorder is the most sensitive to air pressure fluctuations, and it critically reflects both underblowing and overblowing, which produce flatting and sharping. This is especially true of the soprano recorder, and as a teacher, you must have your students concentrate on breath control. Additionally, the students' ability to hear intonation problems must be developed, or else playing the soprano recorder will be disappointing to all concerned.

Breathing exercises can be practiced without a recorder. (Actually, we have been practicing breathing since we were born, although sometimes incorrectly.) Teach your students to take three types of breaths: (1) a quick, full breath with diaphragm expansion, (2) little "sip-of-air" breaths that can be used between short groups of notes (these quick pants help tide over phrases until a place in the music occurs where a full breath can be taken), and (3) long, deep, full, relaxed breaths that can be used before starting to play.

The recorder is a great instrument to aid in the refinement of breathing. The diaphragmatic support, posture, and breath control that recorder players need are within the same parameters as those required for learning how to sing. You will find that you can do much to improve class singing by teaching the breathing basics necessary for recorder.

Look at the songs that you intend to use in recorder class. Decide where breath marks should occur and what type of breathing should be used. This may seem a bit laborious at first; however, it will pay off in helping your students to develop an awareness of phrase structure. There should be a gradual transfer of learning to singing as students begin to habitually "eyeball" the music to locate places to breathe. Musical interpretations will improve as phrases become well-defined and notes are held for their full duration.

Focus of Air

Producing a quality sound on a recorder requires a strong, well-focused air stream. A helpful exercise might be to pretend to blow out a candle from two or three feet away. Have your students shape their mouths as if to whistle. Then tell them to hold their hands approximately a foot away from their mouths. Tell them to start the breath with the plosive syllable "tu" and try to project the air toward the hands. A focused column of air should be felt, but no whistling sound should be heard. You might have them hold their hands closer at first and then move them away. Another approach is to hold the recorder approximately three or four inches away from the mouth and try to blow air into the windway to make a sound—it can be done.

Developing a Strong Tone

Developing a strong tone on the recorder can be a challenge. The lower notes require a large volume of air but a gentle pressure. Middle notes require focused air and increased pressure with less volume, and the highest notes necessitate high intensity with pinpointed focus. Each student must explore each note of the recorder range to determine the correct amount of air that will produce the best on-pitch intonation with tonal quality and sonority. Here are a couple of simple activities that can help your students learn how to play tones precisely.

An Intonation Game

Depending on the air pressure put into the instrument, the recorder can produce a pitch variance of as much as a whole tone. This is especially true of the soprano recorder, as any music teacher who has led a class of twenty-five students playing in unison can tell you!

Obtain an electronic tuner and have your students try to play in-tune pitches. As students concentrate on playing in tune, challenge them to keep the tuner indicator needle steady. Then divide students into teams of one to four players. Have one play while some watch the tuner and some keep score. (Using this approach, you increase the number of individuals involved.) This venture helps students to hear and visualize what intonation problems sound like and provides them with immediate feedback and opportunities for correction. This activity also encourages development of breath support needed to maintain a steady sound and relatively pure tone.

Long Tones

Doing a round-robin "tone-athon" in class can help students learn pitch awareness and how to sustain long, steady sounds. This may be done with groups or with individuals. Have one group start a note and sustain it for four counts. Then have another group enter as you conduct their entrance. The first group then exits (with a cutoff from you, if you desire) and re-enters when group two cuts out. Repeat the pattern for several cycles. Tell your students to try to maintain a continuous sound while intonating accurately. Then have your students do the same

Playing Clog-Free

- Avoid eating before playing. If you must eat, rinse your mouth thoroughly with water.
- Use Duponol or a gentle dish detergent to "waterproof" the windway to help eliminate clogging.
- Make a swab for the plastic cleaning rod that comes with the recorder and use it faithfully.
- To clear the windway, suck back on the beak to extract excessive moisture or cover the recorder window and blow sharply.
- Warm the recorder prior to playing and keep it warm during non-playing periods.
- Use a small piece of paper to clear obstructions from the windway.

thing with their voices (sometimes called "staggered breathing"). Combine both recorder and voice groups. Add some unpitched percussion or barred instruments. Employ Curwen Hand Signals and perform two-part harmony, with one half of your group following your left hand and the other half following your right.

Cleaning and Maintenance

Impress on your students the necessity of cleaning the instrument. Regular care of the recorder pays off, but your students need you to set an example that will encourage them to establish good recorder-cleaning habits. If the windway is clean, the instrument will play at maximum efficiency. See the Playing Clog-Free sidebar for a few quick tips on cleaning and care.

Preventing condensation. There are various anticondensation products on the market that you can pour into recorder windways to help reduce water condensation. Duponol, a commercially available anti-clogging liquid, is one such product. It can be obtained through most retailers who specialize in selling recorders and recorder accessories. Basically, these liquids are detergents that waterproof the windway so that the water beads off. They are similar to the rinsing products you use in your dishwasher. Alternatively, you can pour a few drops of dish detergent into the windway of the recorder and let it dry overnight. You will find that the water will bead off inside the windway. If you use too much detergent and the instrument plays "stuffy," simply put it under the faucet and wash a little out. If you decide to use dish detergent, you will have to repeat the process every couple of weeks, but this method is an inexpensive way of ensuring a clog-free, clear windway.

Routine maintenance. Put a small piece of lint-free cotton cloth in the slot of the plastic swab rod that comes with almost every instrument and carefully push it through the windway. Avoid using too large a piece of cloth as it can become jammed in the body of the instrument. A cloth about 1" x 3" placed in the center of the cleaning rod works on soprano recorders. (I have even been able to put a swab of this size through the bell ends of one-piece soprano recorders.)

One-piece recorders usually do not come with a cleaning rod. If the swab is too large and comes loose from the rod while it is inside, it probably will be extremely difficult (if not impossible) to remove. The best way to clean one of these instruments is to pour a little dishwashing liquid in the bell end of the foot-joint and place the instrument under a steady stream of lukewarm water for a few minutes. This should sanitize it completely. A couple more drops of dishwashing liquid placed in the windway after cleaning and allowed to dry will again restore the water shield and help eliminate clogging. Using the cleaning rod and the detergent and water contribute to optimum performance, in addition to teaching students responsibility for taking care of their instruments.

Lubrication. Most recorders come with a small round container of cream lubricant that is put on the joints of the recorder to allow the sections to fit together easily. Application time is flexible and usually dependent upon the amount of use the instrument receives. It is a good idea to wipe the joint clean before reapplying lubricant. Sometimes the old residue picks up dirt and can be counterproductive to the purpose of lubrication.

Cleaning. Recorders should be washed throughly two or three times a semester. This is a simple matter of placing them in a sink with dish detergent and warm water and thoroughly soaking them for approximately twenty minutes. Wash them out with warm water and dry them by standing them upright with the bell side down.

I wash my plastic instruments with "Dawn" or other hand-dish-washing detergents and allow them to air dry. This seems to keep them clog-free and sanitary.

Wood recorders should be swabbed out after each playing with a cleaning rod and a lint free cloth. Corked joints should also be regularly maintained with joint grease as mentioned with plastic instruments. Oiling a wood recorder is recommended by many, although opinions vary as to scheduled oilings and what type of oil should be used. A local recorder craftsman or manufacturer will usually be happy to provide such information to you. I use a standard woodwind bore oil—many standard products are available from music retailers—and oil my wood recorders once every two months. I use a cloth swab and sparingly oil the bore of the instrument from the head joint to the bell. I then let the instrument dry for a day before playing.

Breaking in a new wood recorder is an important task and instructions usually come with the instrument from the manufacturer. Basically, you play the instrument for only a few minutes each day, over a period of weeks, and gradually increase the amount of playing time during this duration. This allows the wood of the instrument to naturally absorb moisture and is thought to reduce the possibility of cracking.

Moisture accumulation. Water accumulates in the windway of the recorder as the hot, moist breath from the mouth comes in contact with the colder surface of the instrument and condenses. Less water will condense in an instrument that has been warmed up before it is played. The worst thing a player can do is blow air into a cold recorder; this quickly precipitates condensation. A simple technique to remedy this problem is to have your students hold the head joint of the instrument in their hands with the windows of their instruments facing their palms before they begin to play. If your students stop playing for a period of time, have them hold the recorder window again. Besides keeping the instrument warm, it will also keep the number of stray sounds down when you are speaking or giving instructions.

Unfortunately, condensation cannot be completely avoided. Clear the recorder of moisture as soon as the sound starts to deteriorate. A simple way to remove condensation is to suck back on the beak, or cover the window with your hand and blow a quick, fast breath. Condensation sometimes drains down into the thumb hole and forms a water path that cannot be remedied by blowing or sucking. Take the head joint section off, swab the middle and head joint, and put the instrument back together.

Excessive water accumulation is a problem that often results when anxious students become so involved with obtaining notes that they grip the instrument harder, tighten their hand muscles, and usually move their fingers higher off the holes, all of which slow up playing while continuing the salivating/anxiety cycle. The paper recorder described previously is helpful for teaching relaxation. The objective is to approximate a playing situation as realistically as possible. As tension related to playing reappears, call this to the attention of the students.

Particle removal. Tell students that they should not eat before playing. If they eat anyway, tell them to wash out their mouth with water. Food particles become clogged in the windway, hinder air flow, trap saliva, and reduce sound production. If the instrument does not blow freely, try taking a small piece of paper and sliding it through the windway from the head joint side. A thin piece of paper slid into the windway of plastic instruments can dislodge dirt or food particles that will not come out during washing. Moving it back and forth can dislodge food particles that may be hindering air flow.

Note

1. Gene Reichenthal, Long Island Recorder Festival Seminar, 1995.

Chapter 5

The Recorder and the National Standards

The recorder is an ideal instrument for meeting the National Standards for Music Education, especially in the areas of performing on instruments, improvising, and composing (Standards 2, 3, and 4).[1] Not every school has the resources to supply students with orchestral or band instruments, and not every student can afford to purchase such an instrument. A portable, inexpensive instrument like the recorder can easily augment a music program in terms of both quality and quantity.

This chapter is divided into two main sections. The first section addresses students in grades three through six, and the second section addresses students in grades seven through twelve. Both sections provide various exercises, games, and other classroom activities that are matched to the age levels of students and are suitable for helping them achieve success in a standards-based music program.

Recorder Activities for Grades 3–6

Content Standard 1. Singing, alone and with others, a varied repertoire of music

Call and Response. Assign half of your group to play recorder and the other half to sing songs that the class is learning. Then reverse their roles, so that the players sing and the singers play. Divide the group further—sing or play triads, ostinatos, or descants, or do partner songs and rounds. Georgia Green at Baylor University conducted research that supports utilizing a child's voice model as a good pitch-matching source.[2] The recorder sound comes close to this sound. The timbre, unforced sound, and treble pitch of the recorder can be utilized as a near-approximate imitative voice model for pitch matching. Have some children sing a note or a pattern of notes. Then have others match the tones by "singing" through the recorder to match the sounds or songs. (The sound from the recorder will be fuzzy.)

Content Standard 2. Performing on instruments, alone and with others, a varied repertoire of music

A "Recital" Experience. Allow a certain amount of time during each class for one or more students to play for the others. Provide varied accompaniments with rhythm instruments, CDs, piano, or synthesizer. Involve as many students as possible. See if you can incorporate recorder playing into songs that represent diverse genres or cultures from your series books.

Content Standard 3. Improvising melodies, variations, and accompaniments

Musical Questions and Answers. Develop ostinatos for your students to play on Orff instruments. Divide your group so that some students play the recorder while others accompany them using ostinatos. Then play musical questions on your recorder and have your students respond with answers. From time to time, have students vary the timbre by using different accompaniment instruments. For example, your students could use membrane instruments (drums and tambourines), metals (finger cymbals, glockenspiels, metallophones, and jingle sticks), woods (xylophones, sticks, and claves), and strings (guitar and ukulele).

Content Standard 4. Composing and arranging music within specified guidelines

Scrambling ABCs. Questions and answers developed and played on the recorder can be combined into larger rondo forms. Have students play ostinatos on barred Orff instruments or other instruments, varying the tempos, ostinato patterns, and dynamics for each theme. Notate these examples using student-made color or pictorial graphics to illustrate specific musical guidelines and qualities for each melodic excerpt.

Divide your class into three groups. Have each group develop a question-and-answer sequence for the recorder with or without accompaniment. One or two students in the group may play the question and the others provide the answer. Then have them develop some type of pictorial representation (crayon, watercolor, paste up) to match to their tune. The pictorials can then be placed in order or scrambled for variations. Ask students to vary the organization of these themes. For example, the "A" melody could be used in place of the "B" or "C" melody. Perhaps the whole composition could be restructured. Have students try these options. Then ask students: "Which variation was best?" "Why?"

Content Standard 5. Reading and notating music

This activity allows students to read and notate music that they have created as an activity in conjunction with Content Standard 4 (composing and arranging music within specified guidelines).

Reading and Writing Sounds. Identify a key and meter and develop an eight-measure chordal sequence. Have students develop a rhythm for the sequence and notate it using rhythmic syllables placed above the staff. Place chord tones that students have already learned in each measure, and then have them write the rhythmic notation on the staff combining the rhythm with the chord tones to make a melody. Have students play the resulting tune and give it a name. Then have them decide phrasing, articulation, and tempo. After they have sung the song using a neutral syllable, have them add lyrics. Ask them to show how many different melodies they can make with the same chordal pattern. Since each melody is based on the same chord progression and chord tones, students can play the melodies that they created in multipart harmony.

Content Standard 6. Listening to, analyzing, and describing music

What's Different? Select a composition that includes several well-defined themes, including at least an A, B, and C melody that you can play on the recorder. Play each melody and have students identify it. Then switch the melodic order to A A B A; A B C A; A A A A A B (students like this one), or other variations.

Ask students to identify the changes: (a) through a prescribed corresponding physical response (e.g., raising one finger for the "A" theme, two fingers for the "B" theme, etc.), (b) pictorially from photos you have previously identified and associated with the melodies (c) orally, (d) in writing on the blackboard, or (e) by writing on paper at their seats.

Content Standard 7. Evaluating music and music performances

Your Opinion, Please. Record your class as they perform a song, improvisation, duet, trio, or other piece on the recorder. Have students listen to the tape and discuss (a) tempo, (b) what could have been done to make the piece better, (c) how the piece made them feel, (d) how others who might not have heard them practice the piece would react to their performance, and (e) what they learned as they played.

Content Standard 8. Understanding relationships between music, the other arts, and disciplines outside the arts

The Sound of What You See. Bring a painting, sculpture, tapestry, or other art work to class and discuss its physical characteristics. An animated, visual art form that you might want to consider could be the screen saver on a computer monitor in your classroom or on one of the other school computers. Lead students in a discussion identifying the item's color, shape, texture (e.g., jagged or smooth), and size. Then have students use the recorder to try to portray these qualities by means of sound. Multiple recorders can provide additional opportunities for creating a harmonized sound collage or other ensemble activity. Have students experiment with obtaining different sounds from the recorder. (The head joint can produce sounds by itself if it is removed from the instrument, and the sound can be varied by closing the opening halfway as you blow through the windway.)

Content Standard 9. Understanding music in relation to history and culture

Music Here and There. Have students listen to examples of Native American tribal flute playing (see Chapter 9 for some suggested Native American music pieces). Discuss how this playing differs from the way the recorder is usually played today. Use some of the following questions: How are the flutes of Native American tribes different from our recorders? How are they the same? How did Native American children learn to play the flute? Were there music teachers who taught them music? What was the role of the musician in the Native American tribe? What is the role of the musician in our society today? What was music used for in the Native American tribes? What is music used for today in our school? In our town?

Recorder Activities for Grades 7–12

Content Standard 1. Singing, alone and with others, a varied repertoire of music

Recorders and Voices. Develop two- or three-part singing/playing activities in your secondary general music classes. Assign voices to two of the parts and allow recorders to play the third. SAT trios played by members of your class can provide a good background for singing activities by the rest of your class in lieu of keyboard accompaniment. Or, assign a number of recorders to each voice of two-part songs and have them back up and support the pitch of the singing. Because the instruments generally do not overpower the singers, both groups must listen and sing or play accurately to achieve balance and intonation.

Content Standard 2. Performing on instruments, alone and with others, a varied repertoire of music

A Classroom Concert. Provide a library of recorder solos for your general music class students and others involved in the music program. Help interested students to select and practice a piece for a solo recital day. Over time, the library can be expanded to include trios, quartets, and a variety of other mixed ensembles. Incorporating Standard 6 (listening to, analyzing, and describing music), discuss the works performed in terms of their form, meter, rhythm, tonality, harmony, and historical background.

Another possibility is to create three-part arrangements of accompaniments for songs that students like to sing in class. To ensure the playability of the arrangements, write specifically for the abilities of students in your own classes. Alternatively, use recorder accompaniment for one or more verses of a choral selection. Use the harpsichord setting on an electronic keyboard as a timbral foil to accompany a three-part recorder ensemble. Electronic string sounds and percussion patches can also enhance trios. Including parts for unpitched percussion instruments, such as maracas, hand drums, and claves, provides additional playing opportunities and can stimulate students' interest in the music.

Content Standard 3. Improvising melodies, variations, and accompaniments

A Touch of Jazz. There are many fine jazz instruction books available. The series by Jamey Abersold, *How To Play Jazz and Improvise,* is an excellent source for secondary school students interested in approaching jazz on the recorder. These tunes are a good challenge for secondary students who want to learn to improvise. The series provides a CD with a backup of drums, keyboard, and bass, and a well-written, explanatory manual. In addition to other chord progressions, there is a "Blues in F" that students seem to particularly enjoy. A second book, *Nothin' but Blues* (beginning/intermediate level), contains blues tunes in a various keys and is used at many adjudication festivals to evaluate the improvisation abilities of students competing for positions in county or all-state jazz ensembles. Many other books include song charts and accompaniment CDs and a variety of standard songs.

Froseth's "Do It! Play Recorder" series offers a number of interesting blues backgrounds on CD specifically oriented toward recorder improvisation to interest and attract secondary school students. The method book includes clear explanations and exercises for the beginning improvisers.

To meet your students' individual musical abilities and proficiency levels, develop a series of chord progressions and play or record them on piano or synthesizer. Provide notation for the progression and have your students improvise over it. Examples might include twelve-bar blues patterns—I, I, I, I, IV, IV, I, I, V, IV, I, I; "heart and soul" patterns such as I, VI, IV, V7, I; minor patterns—i, iv, V7, i; or patterns with form—(A) I, I, V7, I; (B) I, IV, V7, I; (A) I, I, V7, I. Stay within the keys of C and G for C recorders and within F and C for F instruments.

Content Standard 4. Composing and arranging music within specified guidelines

Theme and Variations. An interesting round-robin composition technique involves creating a simple tune and then having each student add variations. A tape recorder helps to remind students of the tunes as they occur. Have your students create a pentatonic melody on a soprano recorder using B, A, G, E, D. Play it several times for the class, notate it on the board, and record the tune and the rest of the session. Then have your class play the melody frequently enough to familiarize themselves with notes and structure. Next have a student play the melody and change it in some manner. Go around the class, with each student playing what the preceding student has played and then adding to the result. Have everyone in the class try to play the final melody. Play the tape and have students determine how and what was done to make each variation different. What was changed? Melody? Rhythm? Tempo? Articulation? Have students try to notate the final version and compare it with the original.

Two additional approaches to helping students to start composing include using computer and music notation software such as "MusicTime Online," which can be downloaded free from www.notationstation.net. First, provide students with a basic chord progression template to work with including key, meter, number of measures, form, and the notes that they know how to play. Alternatively, explain how to use the software and allow them to compose their own compositions, with the stipulation that they have to be able to perform them. (At some point, creativity has to be manifested practically. Staying within their own playing ability provides students with realistic guidelines and challenges them to learn more in order to compose more.) They may use either alto or soprano recorders. Some students at advanced levels may wish to try writing for the tenor or bass.

Have the students print out their compositions and practice them either in class or at home. The composers can then perform their works in class. They can explain why they composed their pieces as they did, and a constructive discussion can be developed about what occurred in the composition and how the piece could be improved.

Content Standard 5. Reading and notating music

Getting Creative. Have your students notate their own recorder compositions with a music notation or sequencing software package. Many of the new ones retail for approximately $70 and have options that allow for both notation and limited MIDI sequencing with MIDI keyboard or computer keyboard input. Check out gvox.com and their NotationStation page, where you can obtain MusicTime free. Also new and free is Finale Note Pad, which can be located through Coda at www.coda music.com/coda/download_file.asp?download_target=np2k1win. Opcode has a new product for Mac format called Fermata. Information may be located at www.opcode.com/products/ fermata.

It is challenging for students to learn a new program. However, with this new knowledge, students can notate their compositions, edit them, and print out copies of their work to share with others. This newly acquired ability can motivate students to compose and print more music on their own. Install the software on your classroom computer. If you do not have one, see if it is possible to install music notation software on one of the laboratory computers in your school. Students can access the lab during your class time, before or after school, or during study halls.

Content Standard 6. Listening to, analyzing, and describing music

Oldies but Goodies. Access "The Internet Renaissance Band" page at www.intranet.csupomona.edu/~jcclark/emusic/renaissa. html. This page, developed and maintained by Curtis Clark at California State Polytechnic University, is a good site for listening to Renaissance music.

Have your students listen to compositions and dances and develop blueprints or listening charts that detail the sequential elements of the compositions, including the forms used by the composers and the instruments played. Also have students discuss the titles of the various tunes. Note lyrics such as "Be peace! Ye made me spill my ale!" (Anonymous) and "Say what ails my darling" (Morley). It is interesting to see how composers reflect the times they live in through their song titles and lyrics.

If you have a computer with Internet capabilities in your school, this activity can be done as a class lesson. If it is part of a homework assignment and some students do not have access to the Internet from home, set up working groups to meet at homes where such equipment is available.

Thomas Morley (1557–1602) wrote "Springtime mantleth every bough," in AABB form, and it is a good tune to analyze initially. The "Renaissance Band" site also features numerous bourrées and music by Josquin des Prez (1440–1551) and Orlandus Lassus (1532–1594). Have students note "The Silver Swanne" by Orlando Gibbons (1583–1625), listen to the music, and read the lyrics. Discuss the story that the lyrics tell and how the music complements this story. Have students consider the work of Michael Praetorius (1571–1621); included is his series of seven gavotte melodies played individually and then combined in various dance suites. One dance suite combines the first, second, third, and sixth gavottes. Have the students listen to Gavottes 1, 2, 3, and 6 played as a unit (11k, 2:01). After they listen to this several times, have them try to diagram the suite (A, A, B, B, C, C, D, D, B, B, E, E, F, F, G, G, Coda).

Have students listen to Francisco de la Torre's "Alta," one of the first pieces written for Renaissance wind band that included such instruments as the shawm, bombard, and trumpet/sackbut. Then have them research these instruments in an encyclopedia. Ask, What are the modern counterparts of each of these early instruments?

Content Standard 7. Evaluating music and music performances

Music Critic. Ask students to develop a list of characteristics of a good recorder performance. Ask the students to make the list relate to the abilities that they have. Include tonguing, tone quality, tempo, phrasing, and other aspects of performance. Play or have a student play a piece for the class. Use the checklist and see if it covers all aspects of a recorder performance.

Introduce the word "aesthetic." Aesthetics concern artistic qualities and feeling aspects of music. Ask the following questions:

Does a piece of recorder music itself have feeling aspects? Do some pieces of music have more feeling aspects than others? Can we describe them? How are music performances different from each other? Can a performer enhance artistic qualities and feeling aspects of a somewhat poor piece of music? Can an audience or a concert hall make a performance more appealing? How about you as a listener? If you are a recorder player and have tried to play the piece that is performed, are you more sensitive to the feelings being portrayed by the performer? Can you relate to the musical elements in the piece better than someone who does not play recorder? Have the recorder composition played again and ask students to consider the ideas they have just discussed in relation to the class performance.

Content Standard 8. Understanding relationships between music, the other arts, and disciplines outside the arts

Multimedia with the Recorder. Break students into groups and give them the following assignment: Find a recorder ensemble piece and a poem that have similar themes, moods, or titles. Develop a multimedia presentation based on the similarities between them. Use colored transparencies and cardboard masks cut into shapes and place them on an overhead projector as a colored light source. Flashlights with colored cellophane masks to flash on the screen are also an additional resource. Decide how the media can work in combination with music and poetry. For example, what colors or light changes can complement the music theme and accompanying narration (i.e., yellow light for A, red for B, etc.)? Consider the following: (1) By increasing the number of lights, or speeding or slowing their movement, can certain light activities enhance the poetry examples as the words are read? (2) How can multimedia, music, and poetry work in combination? (3) How does the media complement music and speech to make it more effective? (4) How does it detract? (5) Can the light media be made to complement rhythm? Harmony? Melody? How? Try to find ways. Rehearse your presentation of music, poetry, and visual elements. Then present the show to the class.

Content Standard 9. Understanding music in relation to history and culture

A Renaissance Hit Parade. Discuss and research the Renaissance period and how dance was performed then. Have students play and dance to several early music dances such as galliards, pavanes, and bourrées. These can be performed as duets, trios, or quartets. Try to develop a group activity with part of the class playing and the other dancing. Ask students these questions: What instruments prevailed? Why? Do we, or could we, perform Renaissance dances to the music of today? Why? Why not? Try and see. How and why are dances developed? Can you name a dance that developed in the twentieth century?

Notes

1. Consortium of National Arts Education Associations, *National Standards for Arts Education: What Every Young American Should Know and Be Able to Do in the Arts* (Reston, VA: MENC, 1994).

2. Georgia Green, "Effect of Vocal Modeling on Pitch-Matching Accuracy of Elementary Schoolchildren," *Journal of Research in Music Education* 38, no. 3 (Fall 1990): 225–31.

Chapter 6

Teaching Tips for the Classroom

For the sake of organization, suggestions provided throughout this chapter are loosely grouped by students' ages and grade-levels. Depending upon an individual class's progress, however, some of the ideas may be as useful for beginning or intermediate secondary school players as they are for elementary or junior high/middle school players. Included also are tips from veteran classroom recorder teachers. (See, for example, the Tips for Ensuring Learning sidebar.) A section about playing the bass recorder is presented after the secondary school section, because high school is generally an ideal time to begin playing it (at that point, many students are familiar with other recorder ranges, and students' hand size at this age is far more likely to be able to accommodate the instrument). Finally, activities that all age groups can participate in are discussed. These include participating in festivals, working with technology, and solo playing.

The Elementary School Classroom

Third- and fourth-grade students should start with the soprano recorder (C-fingering) because this instrument fits their hand size well. Many fine teaching methods are available, and some musicians have recorded "music minus one" CDs and tapes. Playing along with a quality recorded accompaniment can increase students' listening awareness, which can improve their dynamic balance and intonation skills.

Many ensemble activities can be included in elementary general music classes. Duet and trio books are available for soprano recorders. Orff instruments can be used as accompaniment. Carol King's *Recorder Routes* provides

Tips for Ensuring Learning

1. To become familiar with both the C fingerings (soprano recorder) and F fingerings (alto recorder), I have my sixth-grade students constantly switch between the soprano "brain" and the alto "brain," holding up the recorder and fingering the notes as I sing the note names. I alternate between that and pointing to the written notes on the board and singing, and the students must sing after me.
2. Students are urged to play a variant of "Name that Tune" by performing "head tunes"—a melodies or excerpts of melodies that they have heard and can play without notation. For example, one student might play part of "My Country 'Tis of Thee," and challenge the other students to perform the remainder of the song at the next class.
3. All students have a practice sheet. The student fills in the amount of time practiced, and parents are required to sign it weekly. These sheets are checked each Monday, and students receive stickers if the parents have signed the sheet. Even the high schoolers request a sticker—but they are "special"— they receive the smelly stickers! After four weeks with parental signatures, students are not required to receive the signature (but, of course, must continue practice). These charts, collected at the end of each marking period, are included as one-quarter of that marking period grade.
4. Those students who forget their instruments must play a "virtual recorder." This can be a pencil to simulate the finger positions. While not perfect, the virtual recorder provides a means for utilizing otherwise wasted time.

Source: Sue Riley, South Windsor Middle and High School, Windsor, Connecticut

excellent material for Orff-based activities. You can also develop ostinatos for barred Orff instruments and have your students improvise simple questions and answers over this accompaniment.

Elementary school students usually enjoy playing canons. Dividing the class into two, three, or more parts depends on the students' abilities.

Many introductory methods books introduce the notes B, A, and G first. Successive notes may include low E, high C', low D, and low C. Sometimes D', E', and G' are approached before D and C. F-sharp and B-flat complete the major ninth range. Teaching F is sometimes delayed in the English system. It involves a "fork fingering" (T, 1, 2, 3, 4, 6, 7) where the index, ring, and pinky must come down at the same time while the middle finger is up. This is sometimes awkward for young hands to coordinate; however, it is necessary to learn this note eventually, and one should not shy away from it.

I have found that students tend to look ahead in recorder music books and explore other notes. While we may feel that a specific teaching order is best from an educational sense, sometimes students' enthusiasm and interest accomplish a great deal and can override our pedagogy plan in a positive manner.

There are many references to German fingering in the method books, but many professional recorder teachers strongly recommend staying away from the system. Sometimes students and teacher do not read the fine print, and they inadvertently locate German fin gerings on the fingering chart and try to use them with English system recorders. (According to *The Harvard Dictionary of Music*, "German fingering is based on a misunderstanding of Baroque practice and [requires] its own arrangement of the finger holes.") Check the charts carefully to make sure that you and your students are using the correct fingerings, especially for F.

Many teachers apply "ear before eye" techniques that are excellent for teaching awareness of pitch and sound and correspond to accepted pedagogical approaches. G-E and G-E-A can be used with corresponding Curwen hand signs and can be the basis for singing the syllables "so-mi" "so-mi-la." Utilizing C', A, G, E, D, C as a C pentatonic scale, patterns of these notes may be included to coordinate and correspond with singing lessons and approaches.

The Suzuki Recorder School method books suggest beginning with the right hand notes while covering the upper holes with cloth tape. D, E, and F-sharp are the first notes taught. Additional notes are added as the tapes are lifted; these notes go up to D' and include F, B-flat, G-sharp, C-sharp, and D-sharp.

Do not play the soprano recorder with your group in an attempt to lead your students in playing. Rather, use the tenor recorder, sing, or use a keyboard, because the sound from your soprano recorder will become lost in the masses if you play in unison. Claves or a woodblock are helpful in establishing a good rhythmic beat for tempo accuracy as the attack is sharp, and the duration is short.

Attractive graphics are helpful in assisting instruction in fingering and also in working with rhythmic drill. There are many large-size fingering charts available that you can place on the wall to give students opportunities to view and visually recognize specific fingerings. Try making transparencies that you can use with an overhead projector. (See the Appendix for standard fingering charts.)

If you emphasize the cognitive aspects of notation, you could make notation flash cards, color-coded notes, or various pictorial handouts as a class project to help reinforce the learning of fingerings and notation.

The Ed Sueta Recorder Method includes a series of worksheets in which students are given pictures of recorders with specific fingerings. The student must figure out words from the darkened note fingerings indicated. Conversely, other worksheets include notes written on the staff, and the student is required to color in correct fingerings on holes found on the blank recorder icon placed beneath the notes.

Advice from Veteran Teachers

Martha Miller, music teacher at the Hollidaysburg Elementary School in Pennsylvania, provides several excellent suggestions for classroom playing. They are presented here.

To encourage students to play alone in class without embarrassment, take volunteers first and then encourage those who might feel reluctant to "select a friend to play along with."

To keep students alert and focused on the performance at hand, have one student play a part of the song and ask the class to be ready to come in and continue, or have the class play an intro-

Rubric for Playing Improvement

Teacher Evaluation

	Most of the time	Sometimes	Seldom
Use of Correct Fingering	☐	☐	☐
Playing Accuracy	☐	☐	☐
Correct Fingering	☐	☐	☐
Makes an Effort	☐	☐	☐

Student Self-evaluation

	Most of the time	Sometimes	Seldom
Use of Correct Fingering	☐	☐	☐
Playing Accuracy	☐	☐	☐
Correct Fingering	☐	☐	☐
Makes an Effort	☐	☐	☐

Source: Martha Miller, music teacher, Hollidaysburg Elementary School, Hollidaysburg, Pennsylvania.

duction to a song and then have it continued by one or more students. Because the other students have to concentrate on the person playing as well as their own playing, they must pay attention and become involved in active listening to the music being performed.

A "Rubric for Playing Improvement" (see the sidebar) is an excellent way of developing excellence in individual performance and musicianship. The rubric is printed twice on a piece of paper, once for the student and once for the teacher. The teacher scores as the student plays, and then the student scores himself or herself. You will find that students are very truthful and accurate in their own self-evaluations. Another helpful practice is for teachers to ensure that students are courteous and respectful of each other's efforts. (See the Rules of Courtesy sidebar.)

Donna Basile, who teaches recorder at Thomas J. Lehey Elementary School in Harborfields, New York, tells students: "If you can hear yourself more than you hear the others, you are

Rules of Courtesy

1. Nobody laughs or makes fun of others when they are playing.
2. Practice polite listening. When a person is playing everyone listens.
3. Raise your hand and wait to be called on before talking or playing.

Source: Sue Riley, South Windsor Middle and High School, Windsor, Connecticut

playing too loud!" Have students listen to others and watch for attacks and cutoffs that you provide with verbal and visual clues. Hand communication can involve normal conducting motions such as cutoffs, ritards, and fermatas. Verbal directions, such as a count-off ("1, 2, ready, play") or singing along with the group as they play, help to establish group cohesion. Basile provides eight excellent suggestions for motivation needed to pique student interest (see the Motivational Techniques sidebar).

Both Miller and Basile state that the way the room is set up is important for group ensemble playing and individualized instruction. By dividing a class into rows with wide aisles or into small clustered sections, a teacher can have the physical proximity to all students necessary for group control as well as one-to-one interaction.

Miller provides an excellent solution for storage. She uses clear-plastic holder bases with vertical medal rods that allow the instruments to be stored upright and grouped by class. Names written on paper placed under the plastic bases tell each student where his or her recorder is located. Each student is responsible for an instrument, and if the recorder is misplaced on another rod, the student must sanitize the instrument with spray before using it.

The Junior High/Middle School Classroom

Junior high and middle school students with some soprano recorder experience are ready to study the alto recorder with F fingering. The alto recorder may initially provide more of a reach challenge than the soprano recorder. I am sure you have seen students in your classes with finger problems, especially as they try to produce lower notes. Tension and hand position are usually the problems with note production. Because fingers are tense, they do not cover the holes. Then, with poor sound, squeaks, and

Motivational Techniques

1. Hold a class or individual contest for students to remember to bring their recorders.
2. Present awards for good recorder playing, and report the names of the winners to the school or PTA newsletter.
3. Demonstrate other sizes of the recorder. Inform the class about the history and worldwide use of the recorder.
4. Establish a Recorder Club whose members can participate in festivals, adjudications, and community performances.
5. Include a recorder part as one of the selections for choral concerts.
6. Put up a bulletin board devoted to the recorder during March, National Play the Recorder Month.
7. Incorporate the recorder into cooperative learning activities.
8. For the best motivation, try to use as many activities as possible allowing every student to feel some success.

Source: Donna Basile, "Recorder before B-A-G," Summer Music Conference, Syracuse, New York, August 17, 1999.

a limited range, students lose interest and do not continue past a few simple songs. Students with small finger spans should continue with soprano recorder instruments until their hands can accommodate a larger instrument.

Some students have reach problems because they try to model their hand positions on those of clarinet players. Tell your students to play with "flat-across fingers," not curved. With this position, the right hand can reach lower notes better, and the need to stretch the ring and little fingers is reduced if the players' fingers are over the holes. Your older students will have slightly larger hands, and the concept of "flat-across fingers" can be more easily explained to upper grades (see Figure 1 in Chapter 4, Hand Position Diagram).

Some beginning students may have the "grabbies"—they grab wildly, trying to produce lower notes, which increases tension in the fingers. Because their fingers are tense, they do not cover the holes correctly. With poor sound, squeaks, and a limited range, they too lose interest and do not continue past a few simple songs. For both soprano and alto recorders, experiment with Katherine White's suggestions (in the Suzuki Recorder School books) for covering holes with cloth tape. By covering holes for the left hand (thumb, one, two, and three), notes played by the right hand can be learned first. In some cases, holes four and five can also be taped so that students can concentrate on playing with relaxed little and ring fingers of their right hands and on producing a rich sound. Removing the tape from one hole at a time allows additional notes to be added gradually, and all fingers can eventually be used.

Ensemble activities for upper elementary grades might include alto-soprano duets, thus allowing all students to participate, including those who may not be physically ready to play the alto recorder fluently. Have students with stretch problems at least say and finger the alto notes as others play them, or have them play and finger them on the soprano recorder to produce harmony at the interval of a fifth or "organum." Repertoire for trios of two soprano recorders and an alto recorder, as well as duets and trios for the alto recorder alone, can provide variety and challenge. Interesting materials are available at all levels of difficulty. *Madrigals, Madrigals, Madrigals*, transcribed by Johannes Koulman, is a collection to look at.

Numerous other volumes of trios that provide good ensemble opportunities are available for instruction and performance. There are many ensemble schemes that you might use, such as SSA, AAA, SAT, and SSS. Trios allow you the freedom to use the instruments currently available, should you not have a bass or even a tenor recorder. Divide your class into thirds or try to develop groups with two players on each part. In a class of thirty students, you will have a total of five groups. This small group size is relatively manageable and might aid in class management should you want to try to have all groups practice in your music room at the same. Percussion or keyboard backgrounds are possible creative enhancements.

If you want to try improvisation with your junior high or middle school students, consider the Jim Tinter compositions "Big Mouth Blues" and "A Minor Melody." The CD that comes with these tunes provides information about ways to improvise, and there are opportunities for interactive learning on the CD as Tinter talks to the students and demonstrates examples for them to follow.

"Big Mouth Blues" provides opportunities for an ensemble featuring recorder, flute, keyboard, malleted instruments, and guitars. There are written and recorded solo exercises, patterns, and accompaniment tracks for improvisation practice. In addition to a step-by-step tutorial, there is a license allowing the teacher to copy parts, and the tunes may be used at all grade levels.

"A Minor Melody" is devoted specifically to the recorder and has four-note melodies with an optional second part. Thirty minutes of instruction are devoted to recorder on the accompanying CD.

The Secondary School Classroom

Secondary music classes can be enhanced through performance-centered activities with SATB recorder ensembles. Music appreciation, theory, and arts-related courses now offered by many high schools can all benefit from recorder performance. At the secondary level, physical problems associated with hand size gradually diminish, and students become curious about playing and comparing the instruments in the "full consort" (all the instruments of the recorder family, including tenor and bass recorders).

Ensemble playing allows exploration of music literature and helps to improve tonal and rhythmic awareness. Cooperation and interaction become overt and required. Students participate in realistic, active learning that fosters socialization and communication, as well as musical perception, and each student hears tones in relationship to other parts and must conceptualize and improve his or her own intonation.

When beginning SATB ensembles, have students review alto and soprano recorder parts. Then, for each class, you can have one "brave soul" play the bass recorder and another play the tenor recorder (the number of volunteers will increase each time you call for them). Initially, you may wish to write out bass clef parts in treble clef. However, encourage the bass recorder player to learn how to read the bass clef. It is well worth the effort. Many of your boys will eventually need to be able to read the bass clef for chorus. Select simple four-part chorales (Sweet Pipes has some available), or arrange your own and play four-part compositions. If you select or arrange tunes that your class or chorus can sing, you can provide variety and interest to your class and develop possible concert performances.

Obviously, an ensemble consisting of one bass, one tenor, twelve alto, and fourteen soprano recorders sounds unbalanced. However, your initial endeavors will result in everyone experiencing the SATB consort. It's fun then to develop small groups within your classes and have them practice and perform a chamber music recital for their peers or as part of a school program. Certainly you need to develop an assignment procedure for sharing the bass and tenor recorders.

Demystifying the Bass Recorder

Because of its harmonic complexity and cohesiveness of blend, a bass recorder ensemble (which consists of three or more basses) produces a unique musical timbre that is better experienced than described. The fresh, unusual timbral quality generates and maintains listeners' interest, as does the somewhat unusual appearance of the bass. Because bass recorders allow for a wide range of technical dexterity, many styles of music from easy to demanding can be accommodated.

The bass recorder can give your students a chance to develop recorder ensembles that make full use of the recorder family of instruments. Unfortunately, this is not common practice, but the purchase of a bass recorder can provide an added dimension to your program. I have found in my teaching that this instrument is of special interest to boys and can motivate and challenge middle and secondary school students.

The bass recorder has an identity of its own. The person playing bass recorder must have a secure sense of pitch and rhythm and be able to play independently and hold a part. Notes have to be prepared a little earlier because of the instrument's lower tones. Players should learn to anticipate entrances in order to start with other players.

Fingering Differences

While bass recorder fingering (in F) is almost identical to that of alto fingering, there are some differences. Playing E-flat as if one were playing it on alto recorder (T, 1, 3, 4) is out of tune on a bass recorder. Substituting T, 1, 3 or T, 1, 3, 5 or T, 2, 3, 4, 6 is usually necessary. Producing the lower tones requires a lot of gentle air, necessitating the practice of long tones and careful articulation to provide a solid attack without overblowing to a harmonic.

Knick, Direct Blow, or Bocal Basses?

Bass recorders are available with a "knick" neck (mitered at a slight angle), direct blow (a person blows directly into the cap of the recorder), or bocal (a metal tube like that of a bassoon that connects into the top of the recorder cap and extends down so that the player can blow into the instrument). The mitered bass recorder allows for easier hand reach and uses a neck strap. I like the knick bass recorder because it is easier for a person of smaller stature to play.

Adapting Already-in-Place Thumb Rests

Many bass recorders come with thumb rests already molded in plastic. If the rest is too high and a person using a neck strap is too dependent upon it, the hand will be continually out of position and the player will have problems playing lower notes. To remedy this situation, locate the optimal thumb position for playing the notes comfortably and accurately and mark its location with magic marker or liquid correction liquid. Cut one or more pieces of cork that can be glued on the bottom of the thumb rest to serve as a more accurate guide for the right-hand thumb location. Glue the cork in place (with Crazy Glue or a similar adhesive) to help the student locate his or her hand position, as well as to provide a more comfortable place to balance the recorder. A better solution is the bass peg because it greatly enhances the ease of holding this instrument and assists in providing freedom for relaxed hand position during playing.

Activities for All Age Groups and Skill Levels

Ensemble Consort Activities. Arrangements for small ensembles that include mixed combinations of the recorders (sopranino, soprano, alto, tenor, bass, great bass in c, and contra bass) are plentiful, exciting, and interesting. In addition to traditional classical compositions from all periods, arrangements of "Stars and Stripes Forever," "Hallelujah Chorus," "Take Five," and "The Waltz of the Flowers" provide variety and contrast for young performers and their audiences.

Recorder Festivals. A festival allows students to meet, communicate, make new friends, and share music with their peers, which is helpful for motivation and interest. Besides the excitement of a festival atmosphere, students also can perform in festive ensemble activities that may not be provided in their own district because of scheduling problems or inadequate numbers of students to play ensemble literature.

Public school music teachers should consider the possibility of developing a recorder festival. In addition to the annual Connecticut Recorder Festival, which is described in the School Recorder Programs in Action sidebar, a second example to model is the SCMEA annual Gene Reichenthal Day of Recorder in Long Island, New York, which provides opportunities for students from districts in two counties and private schools (see Figure 1, Sample Program for Gene Reichenthal Day of Recorder).

School Recorder Programs in Action

Timothy Edwards Middle School in South Windsor, Connecticut, has approximately 1200 sixth, seventh, and eighth graders. All of them are required to participate in at least one of four music programs: orchestra, band, chorus, and recorder. If a student does not select a performance ensemble, he or she is placed in a general music class that meets once every three days. Each performing group rehearses daily as a large ensemble, and each has a sectional that rehearses once every three days. Each grade has its own concert twice a year. All classes are graded quarterly with a grade of A, B, C, D, or F. Grades are based on 25 percent for homework (which includes practice), 25 percent for class performance, 25 percent for individual performance, and 25 percent for tests and quizzes. The sixth- through eighth-grade recorder program has a total of eighty students—forty in sixth grade, twenty in seventh grade, and twenty in eighth grade. Sixth graders learn to play recorders, with seventh and eighth graders performing on soprano, alto, tenor, and bass recorders. Music selections range from Renaissance to ragtime. All eighth-grade performing groups participate in a local adjudication. The eighth-grade recorder ensemble has earned the gold medal four out of the past five years.

The South Windsor High School Recorder Ensemble currently has eighteen students participating for graduation credit (1). This class meets daily during the school day, with several students involved in independent study because of schedule conflicts. Of the eighteen, only three students are involved in another performing group. As in eighth grade, these students perform on SATB recorders. For the past two years, when the high school drama club produced the musicals *Camelot* and *The Sound of Music*, the recorder ensemble provided pre-show and intermission music.

This ensemble has participated in adjudications in Quebec, Philadelphia, Baltimore, and Niagara Falls, performed in the "World's Largest Concert," and played with the Hartford Symphony in their production of Benjamin Britten's "Noah's Flood." Besides these performances, the ensembles perform in the community throughout the year. During December, they perform holiday selections in local shopping areas and schools.

Sixth- to twelfth-grade recorder students participate in the annual Connecticut Recorder Festival each spring. The day begins at 10:00 a.m. with rehearsals, breaks, shopping at vendors' tables, and lunch, with entertainment throughout the day. The day ends with a 3:00 p.m. concert open to the public. A mailing is sent to all public and private Connecticut schools in early fall, and another reminder is sent later. The deadline is usually in December, with all music sent to the participants in early January. The festival is developed in cooperation with the Danbury, Connecticut-based Recorder Society.

Source: Sue Riley, South Windsor Public Schools Recorder Program, Windsor, Connecticut

Figure 1

Sample program for Gene Reichenthal Day of Recorder

SCMEA 32nd ANNUAL
GENE REICHENTHAL DAY of RECORDER
BRENTWOOD HIGH SCHOOL
BRENTWOOD, NY

SATURDAY, APRIL 1, 2000
10:00 AM to 4:00 PM

REGISTRATION: $12.00 per student

ELEMENTARY GROUP: Soprano only (Easy, but preparation is essential.)

Section 1 - Districts beginning with letters A-G*
Music: ***A Classical Breeze***, C. Fuller (LIRF)
Lift Your Voices (#1 & 3), G. Skeens (Sweet Pipes)
Swingin' Recorders (Swing & Rock), K. Harris (Sweet Pipes)
Director: Corodon Fuller

Section 2 - Districts beginning with letters H-Z and private schools
Music: ***American March***, D. Goldstein (LIRF)
Lift Your Voices (#2 & 3), G. Skeens (Sweet Pipes)
Swingin' Recorders (Waltz & Latin), K. Harris (Sweet Pipes)
Director: Larry Roberts

*Brentwood - Divide district between sections 1 and 2.

INTERMEDIATE GROUP: Soprano, Alto
Music: ***The Teddy Bears' Picnic***, J. Brattan (LIRF)
Moon River, H. Mancini (Sweet Pipes)
Music from Olde England (p. 6, 7, 8), (Sweet Pipes)
Director: Jo-Ann Mastronardi

ADVANCED GROUP: S.A.T.B
Music: ***El Grillo***, Josquin des Prez (Polyphonic)
The Little White Hen, Antonio Scandello (Polyphonic)
Bless the Lord, O my Soul, Ivanov (Polyphonic)
Director: Ken Andresen

ABOUT THE MUSIC: Each registered student will receive recorder parts. Scores, where available (for conducting or accompanying), may be ordered. (See Registration Form on opposite page.)

PREPARATION: No student is to be brought inadequately prepared.

PHOTOCOPIES: No photocopies are allowed at the Festival.

LUNCH: Bring a bag lunch. Drinks and snacks will be on sale.

TEACHERS: To aid in preparation, teachers may purchase one set of music prior to registering students.

For information call Donna Butler 661-4706 or Donna Basile 472-4291.

32nd SCMEA GENE REICHENTHAL DAY OF RECORDER
REGISTRATION FORM

ELEMENTARY Section 1	#_____	@$12.00	$_____
ELEMENTARY Section 2	#_____	@$12.00	$_____
INTERMEDIATE	#_____	@$12.00	$_____
ADVANCED	#_____	@$12.00	$_____

OPTIONAL PIANO and/or SCORES

Swingin' Recorder - Score & CD	#_____	@$14.00	$_____
Lift Your Voices	#_____	@$ 4.00	$_____
American March	#_____	@$ 2.50	$_____
Classical Breeze	#_____	@$ 2.50	$_____
Moon River	#_____	@$ 4.00	$_____

TEACHERS PACKET

Read the section headed "Teachers" (opposite page).
Circle which single set(s) you need. Order accompaniments from list above.

Elementary Section 1	**Elementary Section 2**	@ $5.00 ea.	$_____
Intermediate	**Advanced**	@ $8.00 ea.	$_____
FOR EACH MAILING OF MUSIC ADD $2.50			$ 2.50
		Total:	$_____

Purchase orders are accepted if the P.O. number is given on this form.
Please be sure that your business office promptly mails your order to SCMEA/Day of Recorder.

P.O. number:__________

A SINGLE CHECK PAYABLE TO **SCMEA** IS PREFERRED.

Mail before February 1st to:
SCMEA/Day of Recorder, c/o Donna Butler, 616 Long Place, N. Babylon, NY 11702

SCHOOL GROUPS

Teacher's name:__________ School phone:__________
Building name:__________
Building address:__________
Town:__________ State:_____ Zip:_____
District name:__________ District phone:__________

PRIVATE TEACHER REGISTRANT

Teacher's name:__________ Phone:__________
Address:__________
Town:__________ State:_____ Zip:_____

Credit: Donna Basile, music education teacher at Thomas J. Lehey Elementary School in Harborfields, New York.

Named for Gene Reichenthal, the originator of the festival who initiated it over thirty years ago as the Long Island Recorder Festival, this event allows recorder students from numerous school districts to gather, rehearse, and perform. Promotion and recruitment is done through the SCMEA (Suffolk County Music Educators Association) and local Long Island County Orff Society workshops. Entry forms are also sent to past participants and individuals in the community. Although the festival is sponsored by the SCMEA, it is open to children from Nassau County and students in private schools.

Students meet for a one-day festival, rehearsing in the morning and performing in the afternoon. There are three levels: elementary (soprano), intermediate (soprano and alto), and advanced (SATB).

The elementary group is divided into two sections. Section one includes districts beginning with letters A–G, and section two includes letters H–Z and private schools. Each of these groups plays different music. Guidelines are developed by the school music teachers before the festival, and the registration fee of approximately $12.00 includes recorder parts. Students bring a bag lunch to the festival, and drinks and snacks are sold throughout the day.

National Recorder Month. March is "National Play the Recorder Month," a good chance for your students to participate in another activity in conjunction with Music In Our Schools Month (MIOSM). As an example of what can be done, cooperative efforts of the Kalamazoo Chapter of the American Recorder Society and area schools have resulted in numerous concerts over the years. The most recent effort was a concert in Bronson Park in Kalamazoo, Michigan, during May of 2000.

Using Technology and the Internet

The computer provides an effective way to extend and enhance classroom use of the recorder. Recorder tonal purity is spotlighted by complementing it with contrasting timbres and accompaniment styles from the synthesizer and sound cards. String, percussion kits, space age sounds, and special-effect patches can be employed as accompaniments. In addition, many electronic keyboards have a very realistic flute/recorder patch that can be accessed to fill in missing parts in trios or quartets or provide duet opportunities for tunes in your method books. Use your harpsichord patch on the electronic keyboard as a timbral contrast in accompanying. Tell your students about the tradition of recorder with continuo (harpsichord and viol da gamba—similar to a cello). Play some recordings of Handel and Telemann sonatas that employ this combination.

The *Band-In-A-Box* programs allow you to type chord names for a song into your computer. The program plays back various accompaniments based on your inputted harmony. You may chose from an endless variety including classical, rock, and bluegrass. Tempos may be adjusted to the abilities of your classes or regulated so that students may practice part of a composition at a slower speed and then restore it to tempo as proficiency increases.

Using this program, chord patterns may be developed and played as background for improvisation activities. Since the pattern can be "looped" (played over and over again) during individual question and answer (call-response) activities, the continual playing allows the teacher to go around the room and listen to each student individually. Interesting accompaniments with syncopated rhythms or arpeggios can reduce the anxiety of playing alone in response to the teacher's musical questions.

Internet resources for use with recorder-related lessons provide interest, variety, and new material. MIDI files are available for downloading from a number of sites, and songs accompaniments can be played through your computer sound card. Many children's song packages that include sheet music notation, MIDI file downloads, and ideas for use with Orff-related lessons are available.

As an example, go to "MIDI's for Kiddies: Songs for Children" at www.concentric.net/~Gamba/.Access "The Holiday Spirit" at www.concentric.net/~Gamba/holidayspirit.html. This is located under "Winter Holidays" at www.concentric.net/~Gamba/ #holidayspirit. This site is only one example of the many Internet resources that can be downloaded, including sheet music, MIDI files, and lyrics.

The "Holiday Spirit" song is in notation format with an accompanying recorder part, MIDI file, and directions for this Orff-related activity. There are many other songs for all ages on this site, many with teaching instructions, music notation, and access to MIDI files.

Solo Playing and Literature

There is a large amount of solo recorder literature from all periods. In addition, recorder playing allows for individualization, performance, and musical interpretation that can be a continuation of the music learning outside the classroom and also throughout life. This important activity is sadly neglected. Teachers would do well to collect a variety of solos and make them available to students for both private and class practice and, ultimately, performance in both the school and the community.

Once students begin to achieve and perform, you will find many others who will want to join the ranks. Begin by having your classes study a solo or solos. (This is better done as an upper-elementary or secondary activity.) When numerous students can play the piece alone and with accompaniment, have a short recital. Expand the activity to other classes and offer it as part of an assembly or concert. Since March is Play the Recorder Month, you could include recorder solos as part of the musical activities that you plan to include for MIOSM. You could also have a recorder festival. (See the School Recorder Programs in Action sidebar for examples of how two schools typically run their recorder programs.)

As your students increase in proficiency and learn repertoire, encourage them to look for opportunities to perform outside of the classroom. Recorder solos are fine for use in church services, and many organists and choir directors are well acquainted with the advantages of incorporating recorders in preludes, offertories, hymns, or anthems. Community music leaders may see numerous possibilities; however, they must be made aware that students are developing solos for public performance and have repertoire. The student is generally responsible for communicating his or her availability to play; however, the classroom teacher can help by encouraging players to seek out those who might be able to recognize and make use of their musical achievements.

At the beginning, solo literature can be selected from your method books. Accompaniments can be added later. However, take advantage of the many fine packages available that provide challenging and interesting musical compositions, some with accompaniments and options for percussion, Orff instruments, and synthesizer. Don Muro has developed numerous collections and solos that are attractive to both students and audiences. There are also many multicultural solos available from Native American, European, and other sources. Examples of solo literature from the NYSSMA manual can be found in Chapter 9.

Also look at the Classical repertoire. Collections that include music beginning with the Renaissance through the present day are available. By focusing on music from the Renaissance and Baroque periods, you can bring an added dimension to the recorder, your students, and their audiences as you can explore these time periods through cultural, artistic, and social parameters.

Chapter 7

Using the Recorder in the Orff Classroom

by Konnie Saliba

This chapter focuses on how the recorder can be used in an Orff classroom to help teach musical concepts, to help students create their own compositions, and to provide improvisation activities. Also included is an explanation of the pentatonic scales used most frequently in the pedagogy of Orff Schulwerk and an explanation of the bordun, a frequently used accompaniment. The last section includes songs that hopefully can be springboards to extended activities such as the comparison of major and minor or the exploration of music from different cultures. This chapter assumes the students know the basics of recorder playing, such as breath control, tonguing, and the production of a pleasing tone.

The Recorder Used for Ear Training

It is always good practice to spend a few minutes at the beginning of each class echo playing patterns after the teacher. It is also recommended that the teacher begin each new pattern on the last note of the echoed pattern. A list of echo patterns ordered from easiest to difficult with examples is presented below:

1. Echo play using four beats using stepwise patterns with simple rhythms
2. Echo play using four beat patterns with one skip.
3. Echo play patterns using the third space C to fourth line D.
4. Echo play patterns using the lowest part of the instrument.
5. Echo play patterns eight beats in length (use a faster tempo).
6. Echo play patterns eight beats in length that include more complicated rhythms.
7. Echo play patterns eight beats in length including notes from low C to fourth space E.

Echo Play Patterns

The Recorder Used for Rhythmic Training

Example: Phrases of Rhythmic Notation, Each Phrase Played on a Different Note

- Clap and speak each line of rhythm before playing it on the recorder.

Variation: Notate three to five different notes on a treble staff. Ask individual students to use one of the rhythms above to create his or her own melody.

The Recorder Used for Creative Activities

Students can create musically interesting compositions using a short poem or proverb and just two notes. These two notes could be A–G, or E–D, or D–C.

Proverb

If a task is once begun,
Never leave it till it's done.
Be the labor great or small,
Do it well or not at all.

- To establish the rhythm, ask the students to speak the poem in a natural way.
- Choose the two notes to be used for the composition and ask the students to begin and end the composition on the same note.
- After adding an accompaniment, the composition might sound like this one:

Pentatonic Scales

Using pentatonic scales, five tones without half steps, is basic to the pedagogy of Orff Schulwerk. There are three "Do"-centered scales (major) and three "La"-centered scales (minor). C major–A minor; F major–D minor; G major–E minor. For C to A minor, or F to D minor, or G to E minor, only the tonal centers shift.

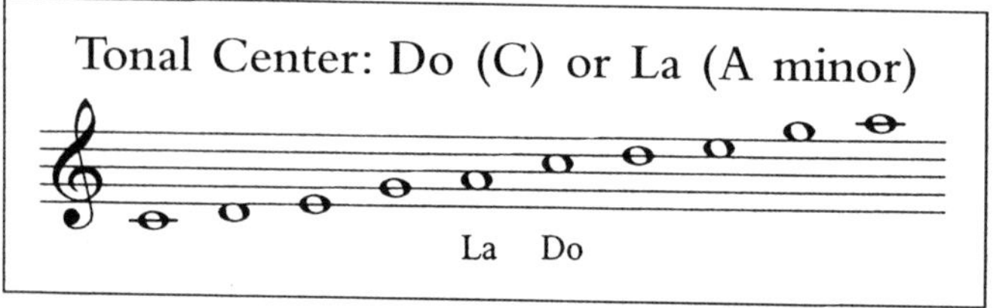

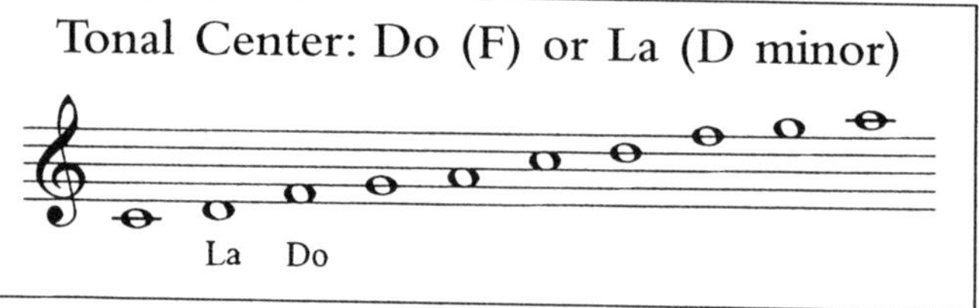

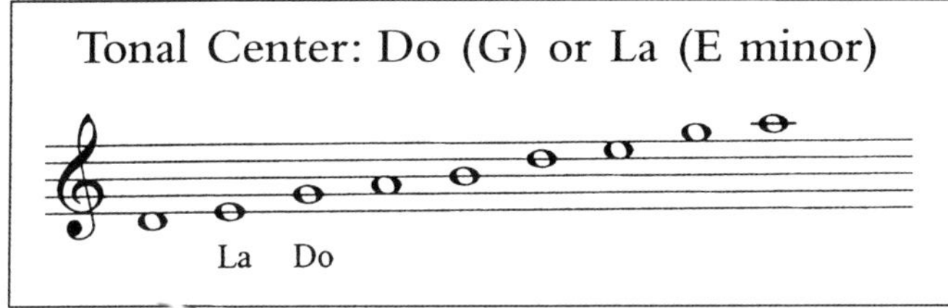

These frequently used pentatonic scales use Do, Re, Mi, Sol, and La, involving no half-steps. Advantages to using these scales are:

- All tones can sound simultaneously, without dissonance
- Melodically, there is no tension in the melodies
- Instrumental improvisation can be successful with minimal training
- There is no harmonic tension
- These are universal scales found in all cultures

By removing bars on the Orff barred instruments, the pentatonic scales look like this:

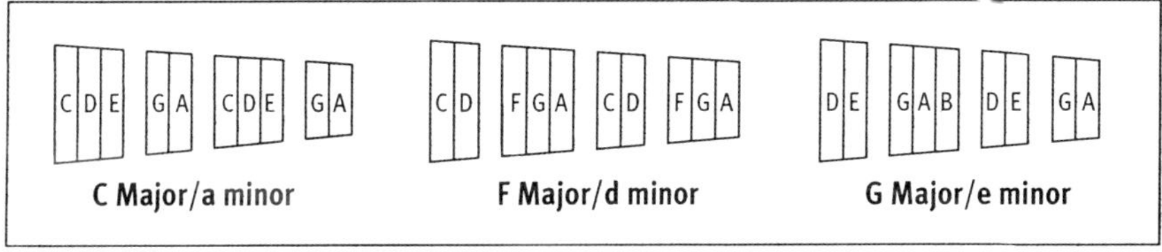

By adding the F-sharp bar, provided with diatonic barred instruments, the transposed D pentatonic may also be used.

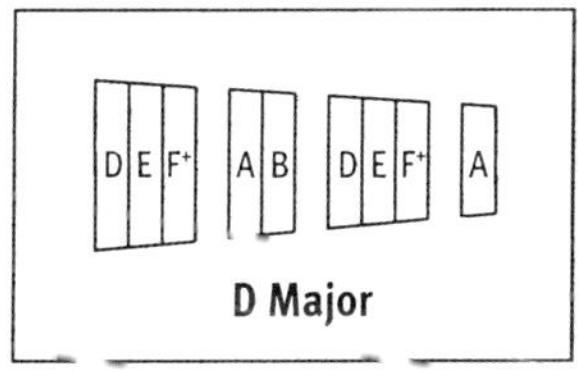

Simple Bordun

Many pentatonic melodies can be accompanied by a simple bordun. The bordun is a single-harmony accompaniment based on the tonic and dominant of the key. The sound of the open fifth as an accompaniment is stable and elemental. Below are four forms of the simple bordun in each of the pentatonic keys. (See also the Recommendations for Using the Bordun sidebar.)

Recommendations for Using the Bordun

- Choose a style of bordun that is appropriate for the melody.
- Put it in the bass instruments so that it is an accompaniment under the melody.
- Play a bordun on every strong beat, or, in the case of the broken and crossover, a tonic on every strong beat, e.g., 2/4 for beat 1; 6/8 for beat 2; 3 /4 beats for 1 and 3; and 4/4 for beats 1 and 2.

Question/Answer Improvisation

When students playing recorder are able to play the notes E, G, A, and B, they can do question/answer improvisation. Using an E-minor bordun as a background for improvisation creates more musical interest for the students.

Begin improvisation in the meter of 2/4, e.g., four measures in 2/4 for a question and four measures for an answer.

Recommendations for Question/ Answer Improvisation

- The questions and answers should be the same length (eight beats).
- There should be commonality between the question and the answer (Another way to say this is that the answer should contain some element from the question).
- The answer should end on a final point or the downbeat of the last measure.
- The question should not end on a final point (Hint: Tell the student providing the question phrase to end with a cha-cha-cha).

The Recommendations for Question/Answer Improvisation sidebar provides structure for the improvisations. However, these activities have to be practiced, and there will be mistakes. Before trying this kind of improvisation on recorder, students should be offered question-answer experiences using body percussion, unpitched percussion instruments, barred instruments in pentatonic keys, and movement.

Suggestions for Question-Answer Improvisation Using Soprano Recorder

Example 1: Improvisation Using E-G-A-B

- Create two visuals. Write the letters E-G-A-B in red on one visual and in black on a second visual.

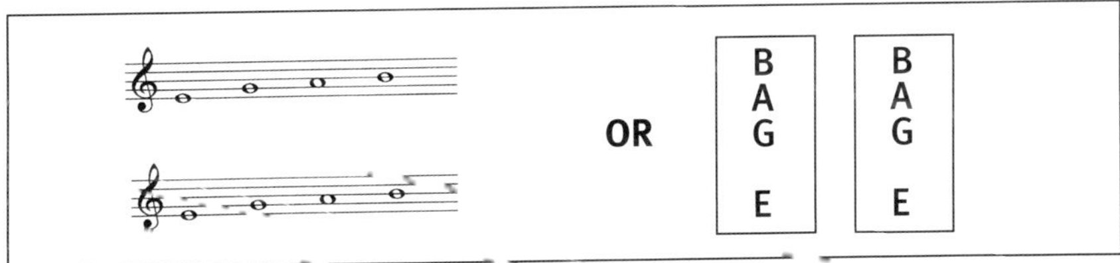

- Divide the class into two groups. Point to different letters on the red visual and ask half the class to simultaneously play the notes with you, making certain you are providing patterns in eight-beat phrase lengths that do not end on E.
- Point to letters on the black visual, making certain to end the answer on an E.
- Select some students to point to the visuals for the class.

Example 2: Improvising from Rhythmic Visuals

- On the chalkboard create two eight-beat rhythmic phrases (See the Sample Rhythms sidebar for suggestions. Phrase one is a rhythmic question of eight beats, followed by phrase two, a rhythmic answer of eight beats.
- Show the notes E-G-A-B on staff notation or a letter ladder.
- Divide the class into partners and practice using the notes E-G-A-B to create question/answer phrases.
- Listen individually to question/answer phrases. Accompany each improvisation on a bass instrument with an E-minor bordun.

Sample Rhythms

- Clap each rhythm to learn it.
- Play the rhythm phrases on a single, selected note.
- Play each phrase on a different note.
- Play the rhythms in a two-, three-, or four-part canon after eight beats.

The Six Pentatonics

Each of the selections after page 75 is in a different pentatonic key, with elemental orchestrations for Orff instruments. These pieces can be expanded to the rondo form by asking students to improvise contrasting sections using the notes in that pentatonic. These contrasting sections could be done in any of the following ways:

- Question/Answer, in partners, using recorders
- Question/Answer in partners, using barred instruments with half steps removed
- Question/Answer on barred instruments, in families of instruments, e.g., glockenspiels, soprano instruments, alto instruments, and bass instruments
- Group improvisation using families of barred instruments for the length of the song, (eight measures) or for half the length of the song (four measures)

Sample Rhythms

1. Q.

A.

2. Q.

A.

3. Q.

A.

4. Q.

A.

5. Q.

A.

6. Q

A.

C Pentatonic Scale

Sea to Sea in C Pentatonic
Konnie Saliba
Claves
Soprano Recorder
Alto Metallophone
Bass Xylophone/ Bass Metallphone
1.
2.

A-Minor Pentatonic Scale

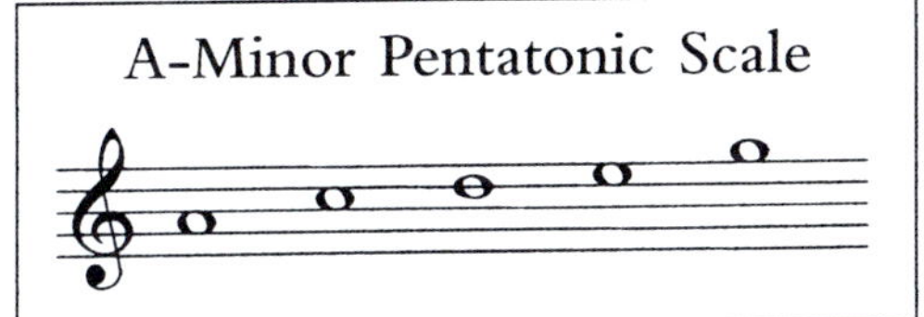

Waltz with Me

Konnie Saliba

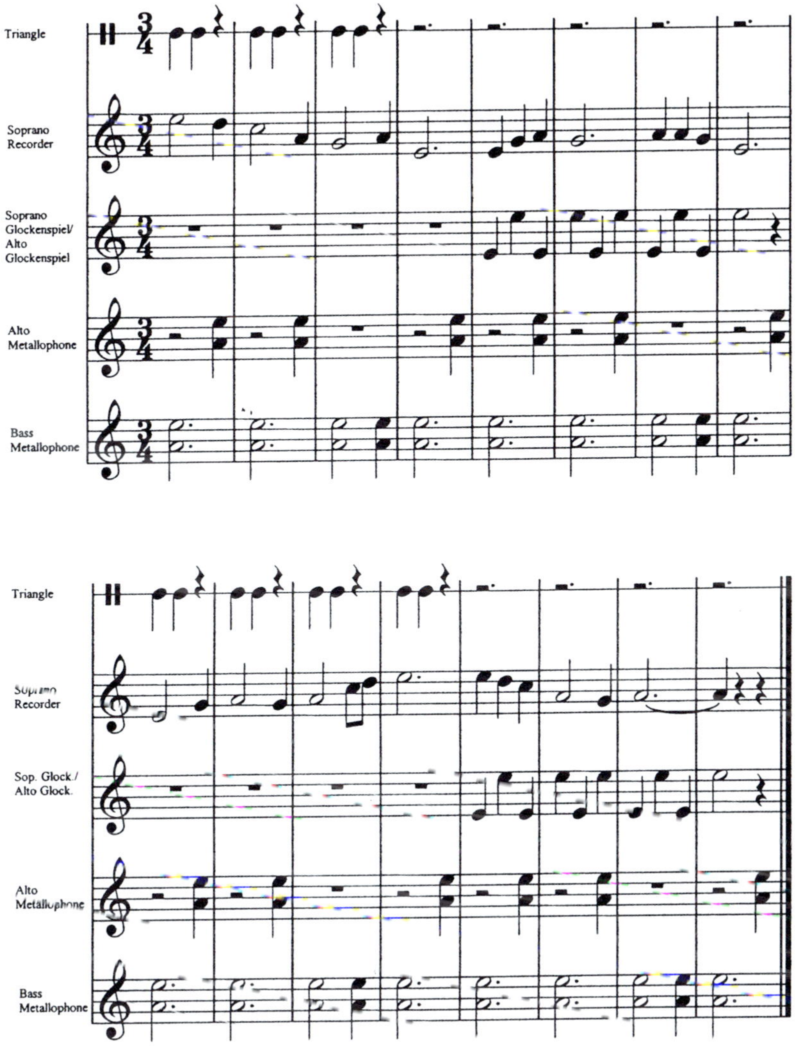

Triangle
Soprano Recorder
Soprano Glockenspiel/ Alto Glockenspiel
Alto Metallophone
Bass Metallophone
Triangle
Soprano Recorder
Sop. Glock./ Alto Glock.
Alto Metallophone
Bass Metallophone

F Major Pentatonic Scale

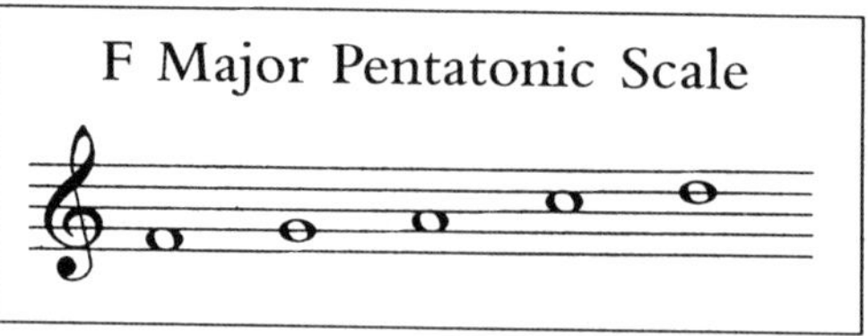

Catch Me

Konnie Saliba

Sleigh Bells
Soprano Recorder
Soprano Glockenspiel/ Alto Glockenspiel
Alto Xylophone
Bass Xylophone/ Bass Metallophone/ Contra Bass Xyl.
Sleigh Bells
Soprano Recorder
Sop. Glockenspiel/ Alto Glockenspiel
Alto Xylophone
Bass Xylophone/ Bass Metallophone/ Contra Bass Xyl.
1.
2.

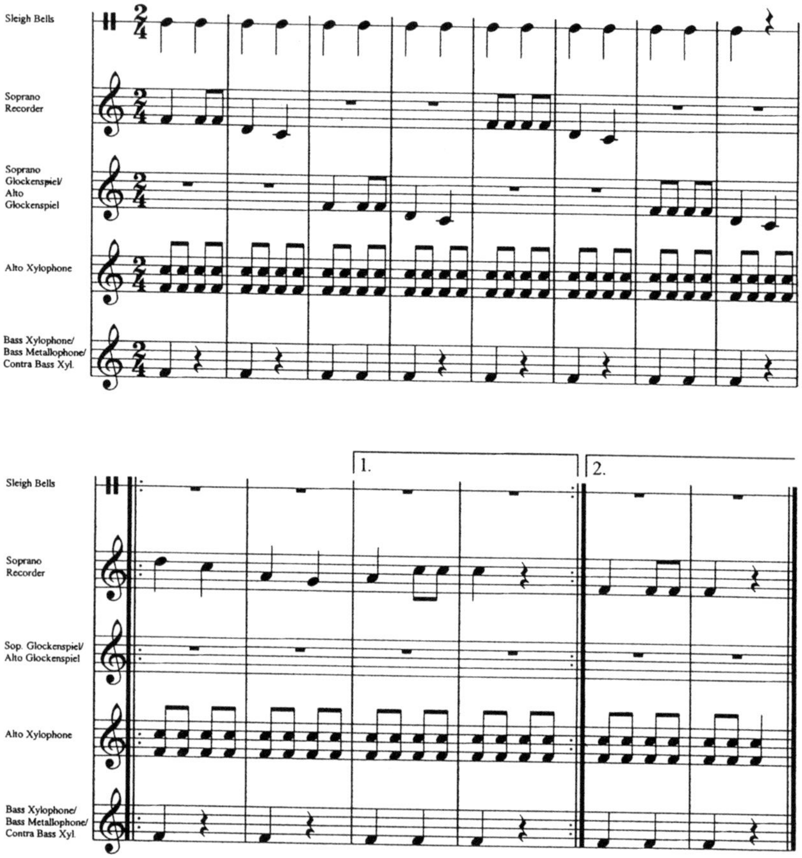

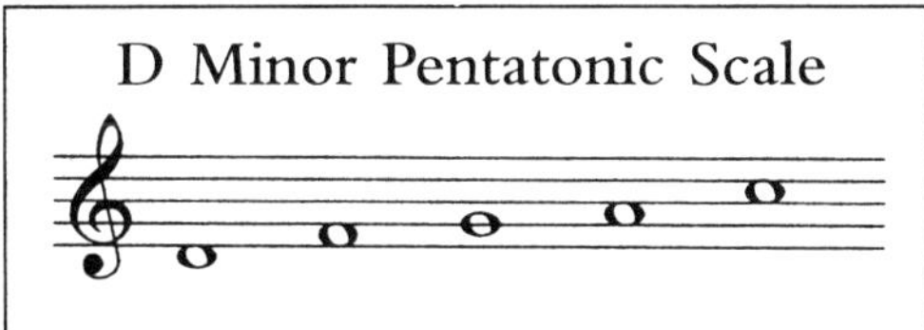

Duet Time

Konnie Saliba

Claves

Soprano Recorder 1

Soprano Recorder 2

Soprano Metallophone/ Alto Metallophone

Alto Xylophone

Bass Xylophone/ Bass Metallophone/ Contra Bass Xyl.

1. 2.

Claves

Soprano Recorder 1

Soprano Recorder 2

Soprano Metallophone/ Alto Metallophone

Alto Xylophone

Bass Xylophone/ Bass Metallophone/ Contra Bass Xyl.

G Major Pentatonic Scale

E Minor Pentatonic Scale

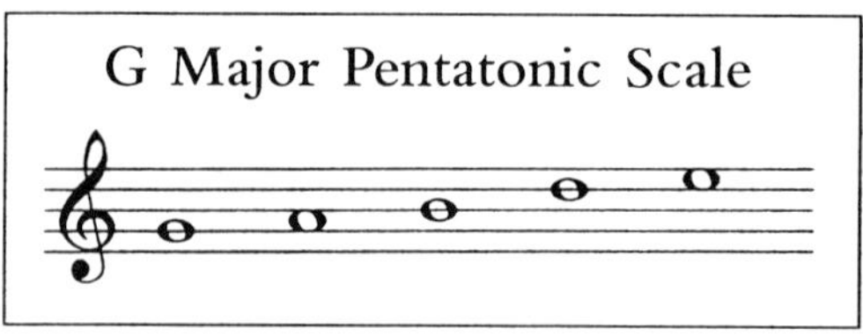

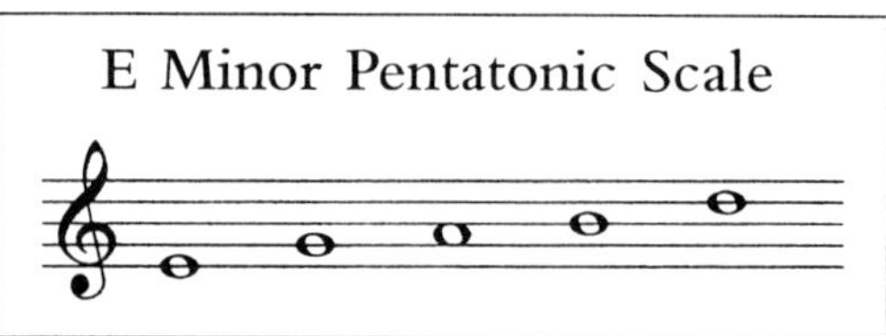

Recorder Fun—Major to Minor

Konnie Saliba

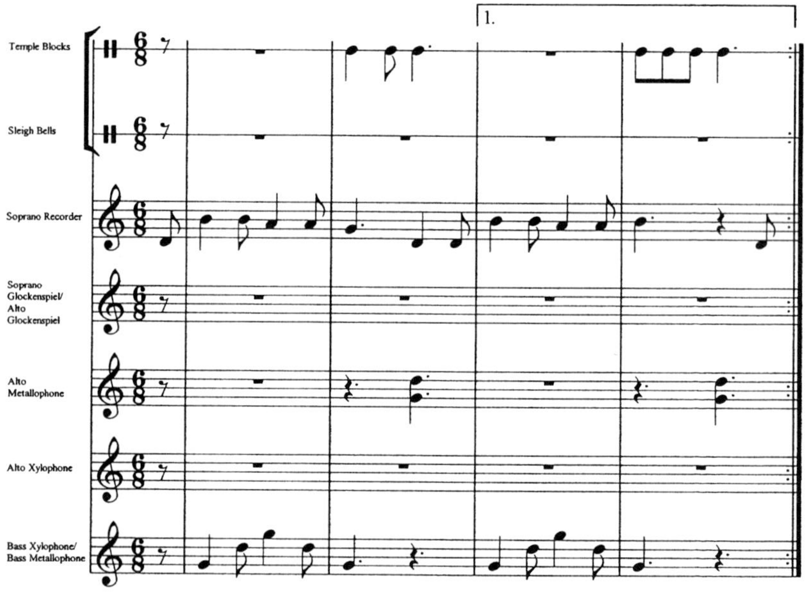

1.
Temple Blocks
Sleigh Bells
Soprano Recorder
Soprano Glockenspiel/ Alto Glockenspiel
Alto Metallophone
Alto Xylophone
Bass Xylophone/ Bass Metallophone

2.
Temple Blocks
Sleigh Bells
Soprano Recorder
Sop. Glockenspiel/
Alto Glockenspiel
Alto
Metallophone
Alto Xylophone
Bass Xylophone/
Bass Metallophone
1.
2.
Temple Blocks
Sleigh Bells
Soprano Recorder
Soprano
Glockenspiel/
Alto
Glockenspiel
Alto
Metallophone
Alto Xylophone

Temple Blocks
Sleigh Bells
Soprano Recorder
Soprano Glockenspiel/ Alto Glockenspiel
Alto Metallophone
Alto Xylophone
Bass Xylophone/ Bass Metallophone

This Little Light of Mine
Afro. American Spiritual
Arr. Konnie Saliba
Tambourine
Voice
1. This lit - tle light of mine I'm gon - na let it shine.
2. Ev' - ry where I go I'm gon - na let it shine.
Soprano Recorder
Alto Recorder
Alto Xylophone
Bass Xylophone/ Bass Metallophone/ Contra Bass Xyl
5
Tambourine
Voice
This lit - tle light of mine I'm gon - na let it shine.
Ev' - ry where I go I'm gon - na let it shine.
Soprano Recorder
Alto Recorder
Alto Xylophone
Bass Xylophone/ Bass Metallophone/ Contra Bass Xyl

9
Tambourine
Voice
This lit - tle light of
mine
I'm gon - na let it
shine, let it
Ev' - ry where I
go
I'm gon - na let it
shine, let it
Soprano Recorder
Alto Recorder
Alto Xylophone
Bass Xylophone/
Bass Metallohpone/
Contra Bass Xyl.
13
Tambourine
Voice
shine, let it
shine, let it
shine.
shine, let it
shine, let it
shine.
Soprano Recorder
Alto Recorder
Alto Xylophone
Bass Xylophone/
Bass Metallohpone/
Contra Bass Xyl.

Hills of Arirang
Korea
Arr. Konnie Saliba
Finger Cymbals
Temple Blocks
Suspended Cymbal
Gong
Recorder/ Voice
A - ri - rang A - ri - rang A - ra ri yo
3
Soprano Metallophone
Alto Metallophone
*Bass Metallophone
* play with stick ends of mallets

2
5
Finger Cymbals
Temple Blocks
Suspended Cymbal
Gong
Recorder/ Voice
A - ri - rang Ko gae ro nau - mau - kan - da
Soprano Metallophone
Alto Metallophone
Bass Metallophone

3
9
Finger Cymbals
Temple Blocks
Suspended Cymbal
Gong
Recorder/ Voice
3
Na rul pau - ri - gu kah - si noo nim euhn
Soprano Metallophone
Alto Metallophone
Bass Metallophone

4
13
Finger Cymbals
Temple Blocks
Suspended Cymbal
Gong
Recorder/ Voice
Shim___ nee_ doo_ not_ kah soo rah pyong nan_ da.
Soprano Metallophone
Alto Metallophone
Bass Metallophone

Chapter 8

Arranging for Success

Recorders blend well with voices, and it is quite easy to arrange an SATB voice score. Indeed, many madrigals, chorales, and hymns are well within the range of the recorder, and these are good genres to begin with.

It is extremely important to know your students, their effective ranges, and their musical abilities. While it may satisfy you to write challenging arrangements, the major objective is to allow your students to showcase their current abilities. If you can arrange music within the scope of what you are teaching them and work with a limited tessitura, your students will be highly motivated because their efforts will sound good.

Chordal and Solo-Tutti Arrangements

Arranging music for the recorder is relatively easy as long as you remember that, in most cases, you will hear the composition played an octave higher. Try employing ensemble unison passages leading into sections of chordal harmony. Chorale-style writing does limit independent line writing, but your group will sound fuller if you employ mostly unison or chordal harmony. Chordal writing provides an opportunity for students to work on intonation and ensemble playing.

Solo-tutti writing can also be successful for a recorder ensemble. One of its advantages is that it provides textural variation without requiring the students to become too involved in counting multivoice contrapuntal passages. Featuring one of the instruments in a section for a short passage tends to make the contrast between the sections greater when the rest of the ensemble reenters. An alternative to using a single instrument is doubling the melody with soprano and tenor or alto and bass recorders. At the distance of an octave, this combination gives stronger definition to the melody.

Transposition Basics

Transposition is simple if you can remember that soprano, sopranino, and bass recorders sound one octave higher than written, and alto and tenor recorders sound at written pitch. Since the tenor recorder is fingered in the same way that a soprano recorder is, present the instrument as an adventure for one or more students in each class, or play the tenor part yourself and divide students proportionally on soprano and alto parts.

"America" Arranged for Recorder

The following examples (Figure 1, "America" SATB as Written, and Figure 2, "America" Arranged for Recorder) present "America" written traditionally and then arranged for recorder. Note that both the tenor and the alto parts are written an octave higher so that they can be positioned in their proper harmonic perspective between the bass and soprano parts. Many players learn to play "alto up, " meaning to read an octave higher. Experienced alto and tenor players can read most SATB scores at sight as long as the alto and tenor parts are played an octave higher.

Figure 1
"America" SATB as written
Standard Four-Part Version

Figure 2

"America" arranged for recorder

Transposed for Recorder

Range Diagrams

Bass recorder players use F fingering, which is the same as that of the alto recorder, and read bass clef. Bass recorder parts sound one octave higher than they are written (Figure 3, The Range of the Bass Recorder). Tenor recorder sounds at written pitch and uses soprano recorder fingering (Figure 4, The Range of the Tenor Recorder). Alto recorder sounds at pitch (Figure 5, The Range of the Alto Recorder). Soprano recorder sounds an octave higher than written (Figure 6, The Range of the Soprano Recorder). Sopranino recorder is excellent for accentuating a melodic line. It sounds an octave above the written note, uses F fingering, and can play any of the music written for alto recorder (Figure 7, The Range of the Sopranino Recorder).

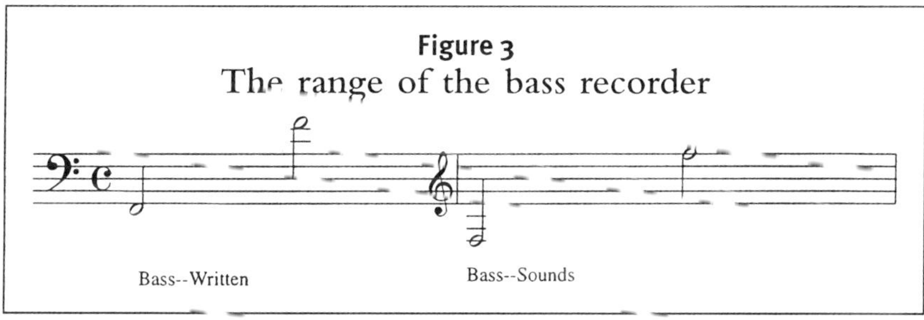

Figure 3

The range of the bass recorder

Figure 4
The range of the tenor recorder

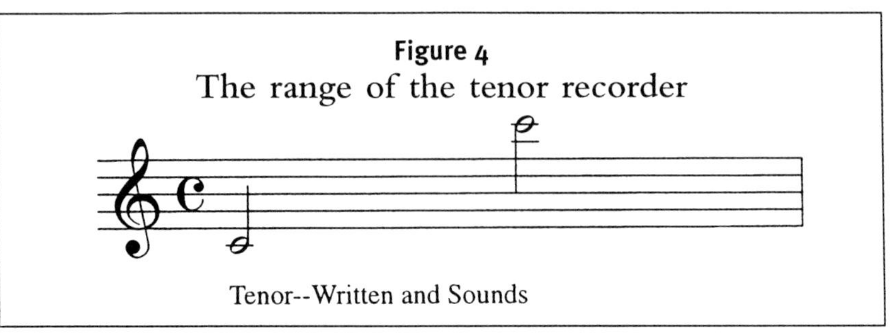

Figure 5
The range of the alto recorder

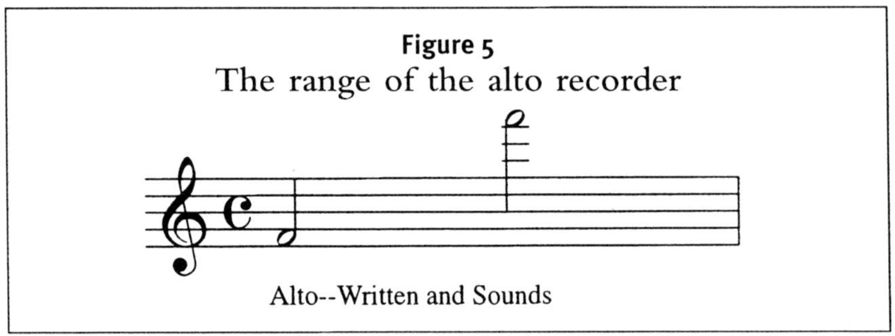

Figure 6
The range of the soprano recorder

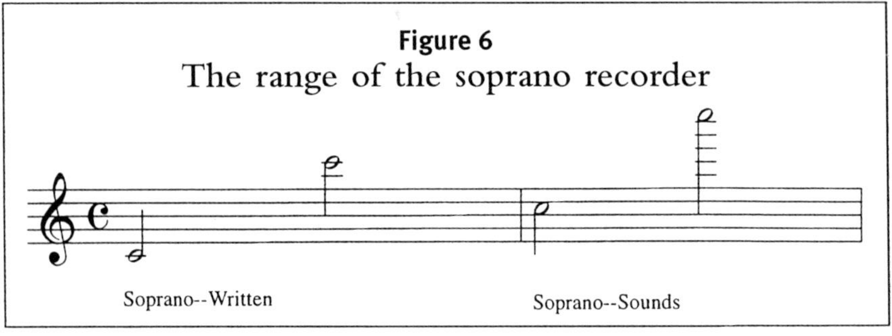

Figure 7
The range of the sopranino recorder

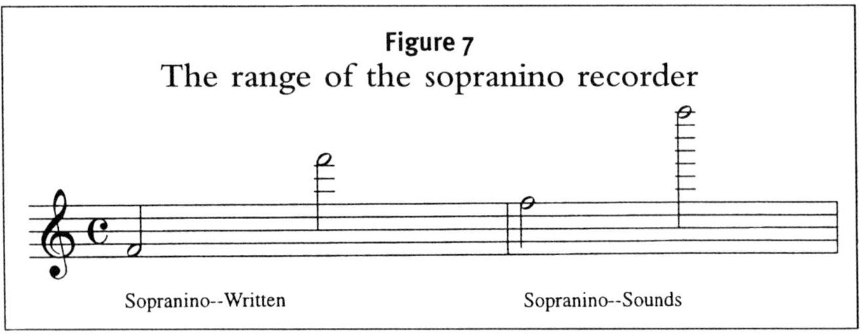

Key Limitations

Certain keys are easier to play on the recorder and sound more sonorous than other keys. The key of F is effective because it allows a solid foundation of lower notes from the bass, and F instruments can play a full two octaves. This is also true for the key of G.

Multiple flat and sharp keys can be difficult to play. Young players are required to cover half of the double hole, which results in weaker sonority. Additionally, many chromatic keys require "cross-fingering," meaning that one or more fingers move down as others go up. Inadequate cross-fingering produces blurring key clicks, which produce spurious partial notes.

Tessitura

There are two octaves of notes on the recorder that can be used for arranging: (1) soprano and tenor c-c", and (2) alto, and bass f-f". Two octaves are optimal for secondary school students. Less experienced or younger students in grades three through six will do better if the interval of a fourth is omitted from the upper end of the two octaves. Their tessitura then becomes an octave and a half.

Younger students find lower tones on the soprano recorder somewhat hard to play, and they tend to lose volume. The alto recorder is relatively stable throughout its range, as is the tenor recorder. The lower octave on the bass recorder is full; however, upper notes can be weak depending on the model of instrument you have purchased.

When you are arranging, try to stay within the two-octave limitation for secondary-level students and the octave and one-half range for students in grades five and six. Many methods books for grades three and four are within the interval of a ninth, so it is wise to look at these books as guidelines. To meet the requirements for arranging for recorder, you probably will have to transpose away from the more difficult sharp and flat keys. F, C, and G are all safe keys to use.

Dynamics

The recorder is limited dynamically, but many educators and arrangers lose sight of this fact. Some methods books include a full range of dynamic markings. While it is beneficial for students to understand crescendos, decrescendos, and the various terms used in dynamics, realistically, the instrument can be played only at about mezzo-forte to forte levels.

What recorder players *can* do is articulate. If you wish to terrace a section dynamically, change the articulation. For example, indicate all-legato tonguing for a forte section and then staccato for a piano passage. This contrast is very effective in chorale-style writing, and it challenges your players as they listen and communicate with each other to achieve cohesion as an ensemble.

The Recorder with Other Instruments

If you want to add variety, back up your chordal arrangements with rhythm instruments, synthesizer accompaniments, and percussion. Use them in moderation and work for balance. Your goal is to achieve an ensemble solo with accompaniment, not the opposite. Pairing the recorder with other instruments in the classroom in addition to chording instruments, barred instruments, and percussion can also be successful.

With some restrictions, upper-elementary and secondary school recorder students can play in ensembles with band and orchestral instruments. Because flatted keys are more difficult for less experienced recorder players to play, it is harder to find band and orchestral literature that can be shared. Music written for trumpets, clarinets, and saxophones tends to be written in concert flat keys such as B-flat, E-flat, and F, which essentially allows recorder students to play in C, F, and G. Unfortunately, to play with any of these instruments, the recorder must play in flats, which creates a barrier to participation as most intermediate-ability players have not yet spent an extensive amount of practice time on scales and arpeggios in B-flat and E-flat. Also, because of its limited dynamic range, the recorder is at a disadvantage with its orchestral counterparts—this is precisely why it virtually disappeared during the Classical and Romantic periods. However, recorders and other instruments can still be brought together successfully. Some suggestions follow.

Beginning ***flute*** method books have duets and trios that allow the recorder to play alongside their transverse flutist peers. In addition, beginning band books may have compositions that allow the recorder player to read the flute part, although multiple sharp or flat keys may be a problem.

Clarinet methods with duets and trios written in G are usable because the recorder player can play the melody line in F (the recorder part will have to be transposed down a note). Try arranging some duets with the clarinet playing the harmony line in the lower register and the soprano recorder playing melody. Examine the parts closely for duet or other performance opportunities.

Beginning and intermediate ***violin*** players have a real comrade in the recorder player! Their music is written in the same key and with essentially the same note ranges, and the beginning string player has the same key limitations as the beginning recorder players does when he or she attempts to play along with brass and woodwind peers. These instruments generally share the same dynamic level. Their timbres are unique so that both have individual identities. When they perform, they will not overpower each other. Arranging string and recorder duets and trios is fun to do, and it gives the players of both instruments a chance to perform.

Chapter 9

Literature and Other Resources

The variety of resources for recorder playing is broader and deeper than some may expect. This chapter provides inclusive although not exhaustive listings based on difficulty level, type of music, and solo/ensemble grouping.

Determining Difficulty

Know the limitations of your performers. Assess their ability to work with specific rhythms and notes that they have studied. Are they comfortable with dotted notes? What about more advanced keys? What notes can they play fluently? What articulation facility and experience do they have? Are they able to independently hold a part without help from another player?

The method book you may already be using in your general music classes can give you a good idea about what your students know and can do already. Just summarize what is there, and you will have an encapsulation of your students' knowledge. When you consider which music to purchase, look for specific ranges that stay consistently within the abilities of your students. Large interval skips between registers should be avoided.

How to Evaluate and Select a Recorder Method Book

There is a myriad of materials available for recorder. Be sure to ask publishers and distributors for their free catalogs. Tight budgets necessitate careful scrutiny of specific method books before recommending or purchasing them. Think about specific aspects of your program that you wish to reinforce or enhance through the use of a recorder textbook. Do you:

- want to use recorder activities primarily for teaching notation?
- want to incorporate songs with ethnic or multicultural backgrounds?
- want a text with a musical dictionary of terms?
- want songs and exercises that will complement a specific approach?

The more objectives you can specify, the better you can clarify your needs and bypass materials that do not meet your criteria. The What to Look for in a Soprano Recorder Method Book Checklist (see the sidebar) gives a few suggestions.

Supplies and Equipment

Collins & Williams Historic Woodwinds. Lee Collins, 5 White Hollow Road, Lakeville, CT 06039; 860-435-0051; e-mail: collins@discovernet.net. Web site: www.windworld.com/gallery/collins/. This company provides restoration, repair, and maintenance services. It offers authorized repair service for Moeck, Zen-On, Coolsma, Aura, Dolmetsch, Mollenhauer, and other makers.

Kelischek Workshop/Susato Press. Michael Kelischek, 199 Waldroup Road, Brasstown, NC 28902; 828-837-5833; fax 828-837-8755; e-mail: recorder@susato.com. Web site: www.susato.com. This company publishes recorder music and methods, Native American music for recorder or flute, and numerous methods and music for folk instruments (Kelischek). It sells recorder music from many publishers and provides recorders and service for Moeck, Mollenhauer, Zen-On, Aulos, and Yamaha brand instruments (Susato).

Magnamusic Distributors, Inc. Madeline Hunter, 74 Amenia Union Road, Sharon CT, 06069; 860-364-5431; fax 860-364-5168; e-mail: Magnamusic@Magnamusic.com. Web site: www.Magnamusic.com. This company imports and distributes recorders, historical woodwind instruments, shakuhachi, and harpsichords. It has one of the largest inventories of early and

What to Look for in a Soprano Recorder Method Book Checklist

- ☐ Rounds, canons, descants, and two- and three-part harmony.
- ☐ CDs or tapes. (Tapes are fine, but they wear and change pitch as the tape stretches.)
- ☐ Songs that will complement multicultural and folksong singing activities while providing opportunities for both playing and singing.
- ☐ Songs that will complement seasonal holidays that are celebrated throughout the year and provide supplemental repertoire to basal series books.
- ☐ Opportunities for improvisation. (Chord symbols should be given so that the teacher can provide chordal accompaniments and should be printed in the students' book as well.)
- ☐ Recorded examples in a "music minus one" format. (The tune is presented first as a recorder solo with accompaniment and then only as an accompaniment.)
- ☐ Lyrics for singing.
- ☐ Information about the form and historical and cultural aspects of the songs.
- ☐ A comprehensive teacher's manual with suggestions for performance, note reading, ear training, and creative use of the material.
- ☐ Ear-training exercises in which students are encouraged to play passages or other songs.
- ☐ Worksheets oriented toward notation, composition, and theory exercises.
- ☐ A dictionary in the student's book that includes music terms, signs, and symbols needed for interpreting and understanding musical examples in the text.
- ☐ Genuine recorder music: excerpts from sonatas, dance tunes, and folk music that were written specifically for the recorder.
- ☐ Rhythm charts, scale, and chordal exercises that enable performance of the included tunes and that assist in the development of fundamental technique.

contemporary sheet music available in the United States and Canada.

Rhythm Band Instruments, Inc. PO Box 126, Ft. Worth, TX 76101; 800-424-4724; e-mail: rhythmband@aol.com. Web site: www.rhythmband.com. This company offers Aulos recorders and equipment, Orff instrumentarium, and Sweet Pipes publications.

Von Huene Workshop/Early Music Shop of New England. Nikolaus von Huene, 65 Boylston Street, Brookline MA 02445-7694; 617-277-8690; fax 617-277-7217; e-mail: sales@vonHuene.com. Web site: www.vonHuene.com. The Von Huene Workshop makes and deals in fine woodwinds in Renaissance and Baroque styles. Its affiliate, the Early Music Shop of New England, supplies recorders, flutes, reed instruments, early keyboards, sheet music, and related items.

Teaching and Methodology

Summer sessions for recorder instruction, which take place throughout the United States, are varied and attractive. Classes and activities are designed to include work in early music, recorder pedagogy, and related performance activities, such as madrigal singing, dancing, ornamentation, and read-throughs. These sessions are good places to learn about teaching the recorder, and classes are usually geared to the abilities of the attendees. A listing of these sessions is published each year in the March issue of *The American Recorder.* Most sessions consist of intensive instruction and last approximately one to two weeks. Many of the activities culminate in concerts and recitals, and some of the sessions offer college credit.

Other sources include the following:

Blaker, Frances. *The Recorder Player's Companion.* Series No. 3. Albany, CA: PRB Productions, 1993. A book for both beginning and more advanced players that provides detailed information about recorders and performance specifics.

Froseth, James O. *Do It! Play Recorder.* Chicago: GIA Publications, Inc., 1998. A comprehensive recorder method that includes CD accompaniments to many of the exercises.

Howell, Susan T. *Recorder in the Kodály Classroom: An Integrated Methodology.* Blacksburg, VA: Music House Press, 1995. A well-written text from a professional practitioner in the field that examines the use of the recorder in conjunction with the Kodály approach to teaching music in the classroom. Includes resources and lesson plans, a teacher's manual, and a separate student songbook.

Junior Recorder Society. *Leader's Resource Notebook.* Available from American Recorder Society, PO Box 631, Littleton, Colorado 80160-0631. Primarily developed for working with children, but also a valuable guide for helping students of all ages develop a strong foundation in recorder playing.

van Hauwe, Walter. *The Modern Recorder Player.* Three volumes. London: Schott, 1987. Presents comprehensive information about recorder playing for players at any level of expertise.

Warner, Brigette. *Orff-Schulwerk: Applications for the Classroom.* Englewood Cliffs, NJ: Prentice Hall, 1991. A step-by-step exploration of rhythm, melody, and harmony according to the Orff method.

Wollitz, Kenneth. *The Recorder Book.* New York: Knopf, 1982. A complete and comprehensive volume of interest to all recorder players.

Music for the Recorder

This section presents lists of method books for soprano and alto recorders. Included also are suggestions for duets, trios, and quartets. The *NYSSMA Manual,* which is used as a source for adjudication and festival pieces, is discussed briefly. The titles of a few books offering Native American music and improvisation instruction and exercises are also provided.

Method Books for Soprano Recorder

Burakoff, Gerald and Sonya. *Hands On Recorder* (SP2358) and Hands On Recorder CD (SP2358CD). Fort Worth, TX: Sweet Pipes, 1995. Written to appeal to teachers who follow the Orff approach.

Burakoff, Gerald and Sonya. *Playing Soprano Recorder* (SP2355). Fort Worth, TX: Sweet Pipes, 1994. Written for beginners of all ages, including adults.

Burakoff, Gerald and Sonya. *Recorder Time* (SP2308) and Recorder Time CD, arranged and orchestrated by Alan Arnold (SP2308CD). Fort Worth, TX: Sweet Pipes, 1997. A method book for young beginners. The CD includes instrumental accompaniments for *Recorder Time.*

Crook, Beth, and Gerald Burakoff. *Recorder and More* (SP2342). Fort Worth, TX: Sweet Pipes, 1990. For elementary school beginners. Comes with play-along CDs.

King, Carol. *Recorder Routes,* Books 1 and 2. Lakeland TN: Memphis Musicraft, 1994. Good source for working with the Orff approach.

Sueta, Ed. *Ed Sueta Recorder Method.* Rockaway, NJ: Macie Publishing Company, 1996. Systematic method based on rhythm syllables, rhythm charts, and tactile coordination of the fingers. Includes CDs, activities, games and worksheets.

Thomas, Christopher, and Judith Thomas. *Three to Get Ready.* Santa Barbara, CA: Muse Manifest, 1997. Teacher's notes, students' reproducible sheets, CD, and cassette also available.

Method Books for Alto Recorder

Bonsor, Brian. *Enjoy the Recorder,* Treble Tutor, Books 1 and 2. London: Schott, 1993. Good methods books to begin and continue with.

Burakoff, Gerald, and Sonya. *Playing Alto Recorder.* Fort Worth, TX: Sweet Pipes, 1994. Method book written for beginners of all ages, including adults.

Duschenes, Mario. *Method for the Recorder,* Parts One and Two. Toronto, Canada: Berandol Music Limited. Part One, 1957; rev. 1998; Part Two, 1962. Separate soprano and alto recorder formats for the upper grades.

Orr, Hugh. *Basic Recorder Technique,* Volumes 1 and 2. New York: Associated Music Publishing, Inc., 1969. Separate soprano and alto recorder formats.

White, Katherine. *Suzuki Recorder School,* Volumes 1–4. Miami, FL: Summy-Birchard Inc., Warner Bros. Publications, 1997. Recorder music and exercises. Separate soprano and alto formats. Corresponding CDs containing recorded music examples from text.

Duets

Burakoff, Sonya. *Alto for Two.* Fort Worth, TX: Sweet Pipes, 1985. For two alto recorders with optional percussion.

Burakoff, Sonya. *Duet Time,* Books 1 and 2. Fort Worth, TX: Sweet Pipes, 1990. For two soprano recorders with optional percussion.

Clark, Paul. *Notes Afloat.* Fort Worth, TX: Sweet Pipes, 1988. Easy elementary-level pieces for two soprano recorders and piano.

Muro, Don. *Friends Are Always There.* Sharon, CT: Magnamusic, 1994. For SS with tape by J. D. Wall.

Solomon, Jim and Mary. *The Tropical Recorder.* Lakeland, TN: Memphis Musicraft, 1997. For two recorders, Orff instruments, and guitar.

Trios

Bonner, Bradley L. *Masterwork Themes for Three Soprano Recorders.* Fort Worth, TX: Sweet Pipes, 1998. A good collection for introducing and enjoying themes from major compositions.

Duschenes, Mario. *Easy Trios for SSA.* Sharon, CT: Magnamusic, 1970. Fun and easy trios for entry-level players.

Koulman, Johannes. *Madrigals, Madrigals, Madrigals* (CM101-SSA). Fort Worth, TX: Sweet Pipes, 1973. Includes traditional tunes of the past that are a lot of fun to play as well as to hear.

Muro, Don. *A Touch of Spain*. Sharon, CT: Magnamusic, 1981. For intermediate-level players; four performance options: S, SS, SSA, and SSAT with tape or piano.

Whitney, Maurice C. *Bach For Three Recorders*. Fort Worth, TX: Sweet Pipes, 1995. A good opportunity to experience Bach with three recorders.

Quartets

Burakoff, Sonya, and Willy Strickland. *The Quartet Recorder*, Books 1 and 2. Fort Worth, TX: Sweet Pipes, 1975. Book 1: musically interesting quartets (SATB) with parts of equal interest and difficulty. Book 2: music from Renaissance, Baroque, and Old English literature.

Hassler, Hans Leo. *Eleven German Chorales*. Fort Worth, TX: Sweet Pipes, 1990. Arr. William E. Hettrick. Allows quartet players to experience four-part chorale style playing.

Hettrick, William E. *Sweet Land of Liberty*. Fort Worth, TX: Sweet Pipes, 1996. Traditional tunes, national hymns, and official marches of the United States armed forces.

The *NYSSMA Manual*

The New York State School Music Association (NYSSMA), a state affiliate of MENC, publishes the *NYSSMA Manual*, a listing of graded music for all instruments and performing organizations. Unique to this manual is a graded list of recorder compositions for students who wish to enter adjudication festivals to present solo repertoire. The grading system includes difficulty levels, ranging from levels one through six, and was developed by Gene Reichenthal, who is the editor, a veteran teacher with more than twenty years of experience in public school classrooms and an extensive contributor to recorder education in the United States. Included in the list are solos, duets, trios, quartets, quintets, and miscellaneous ensembles. This list is a source of evaluated recorder music that is currently available and recommended for use with public school children. The latest edition can be obtained through NYSSMA at 2165 Seaford Avenue, Seaford, NY, 11783-2730, or from the NYSSMA editor, Donald

Coley, 116 Community Manor Drive, Apt #2, Rochester, New York 14623 (716-427-8256). Listed below are a few selections from the publication.

Level One:
Muro, Don. *Rockin' Easy.* (S, SS) Merrick, NJ: J. D. Wall Publishing Co., 1989. Written for beginning-level recorder players with two performance options.

Simpson, K. *Twelve for Two.* (S) Miami, FL: Warner Bros, 1969. Easy ensemble pieces for recorder and piano; excellent compositions for level I competition.

Level Two:
Bixler, M. *American Folksongs from Southern Mountains.* (S) Sharon, CT: Magnamusic, 1962. Beloved folksongs in easy settings; fifteen for alto solo, three for alto/tenor duet.

Feldstein, Sandy. *Holiday Song Book.* (S) Van Nuys, CA: Alfred Music, 1982. A collection for all occasions.

Level Three:
Porpora, N. *Sinfonia.* (A) Northport, NY: Polyphonic Publications, 1963. A stylistic composition of the early eighteenth century that provides opportunities for ornamentation. Of intermediate difficulty.

Rooda, G. *Ninety-Five Dexterity Exercises and Dances.* (S&A) Miami, FL: Warner Bros, 1964. A basic, standard exercise book that is economical to purchase and provides dexterity exercises and dances in numerous keys.

Level Four:
Reichenthal, Eugene. *Easy Melodies for Recorder and Guitar.* (S) Miami, FL: Warner Bros., 1984. An outstanding collection of tunes by a master recorder player and teacher.

Marcello, B., and M. Whitney *Sonata.* (A) New York, NY: GMC, 1994. A well-written sonata with clearly contrasting movement and opportunities to display the flexible characteristics of the recorder.

Level Five:

Bergmann, W. *Bass Recorder Album.* (B) Sharon, CT: Magnamusic, 1977. For recorder with keyboard; a wide selection of compositions for solo bass recorder.

Leigh, W. *Sonatina.* (A) London: Schott, 1944. Original music for alto recorder.

Level Six:

Jacob, G. *Suite for Treble Recorder.* (A/Sopranino) Boston, Massachusetts: Oxford University Press, 1969. For strings and alto or sopranino recorder (piano score may be substituted).

Telemann, G. *Six Fantasias.* (A) Miami, FL: Warner Bros., 1974. Recorder solos for alto recorder.

Ensemble Music

The following ensemble music may be obtained from Ken Andresen at Polyphonic Publications, a major arranger of recorder music. It has been field-tested with students in public schools.

Black, Johnny S. *Paper Doll.* Northport, NY: Polyphonic Publications, 1993. For SATTBB (G-flat). Sheet music of moderate difficulty. Classic swing tune written in 1915. Arr. Denis Bloodworth.

Bloodworth, Denis, arr. *A Suite of Early English Keyboard Music.* Northport, NY: Polyphonic Publications, 1994. For SiSSAATTBB (G-flat, C-flat). Moderate difficulty. Six pieces originally written for keyboard including "March and Ayre" by Jeremiah Clark, "Gavotte" by Samuel Arnold, "Sarabande" by Anthony Young, "Rigadoon" by Henry Purcell, and "Country Dance" by Charles Dibdin.

Bloodworth, Denis, arr. *Popular Renaissance Dances.* Northport, NY: Polyphonic Publications, 1995. For SiSSAATTBB (G-flat, C-flat). Moderate difficulty. Six Renaissance dances—two courantes, two pavanes, a galliard, and a ronde—set in eleven parts.

Broege, Timothy. *Meadows.* Northport, NY: Polyphonic Publications, 1994. For SAATB. Moderate difficulty. A mixture of moods in five movements by a new composer.

Broege, Timothy. *Partita Marietta.* Northport, NY: Polyphonic Publications, 1997. For SSAATTB. Moderate difficulty. Originally dedicated to the McCleskey Middle School Recorder Ensemble.

Note: The following compositions have been arranged by Stan Davis. They may be obtained from Arcadian Press in Northport, New York.

Clarke, Jeremiah. "Trumpet Voluntary" (1700). Northport, NY: Arcadian Press, 1996. SATB. Originally thought to be composed by Purcell, this standard is great for liturgical and commencement usage.

Gershwin, George. "Little Rhapsody in Blue" (1927). Northport, NY: Arcadian Press, 1999. SATB. Gershwin and the recorder go well together. This piece is a lot of fun to play.

Desmond, Paul. "Take Five" (1960). Northport, NY: Arcadian Press, 1996. AATB. A well-known tune in 5/4 time with a number of opportunities for solos from the ensemble. A great tune to include on a concert program.

"Hava Nagila." Northport, NY: Arcadian Press, 1999. SATB. A well-known tune arranged for recorder with myriad performance opportunities.

Jessel, George. "Parade of the Tin Soldiers" (1905). Northport, NY: Arcadian Press, 1998. SATB. This arrangement complements the tune well and is a real audience pleaser.

Herbert, Victor. "March of the Toys" (1903). Northport, NY: Arcadian Press, 1998. SATB. A well-arranged favorite for SATB.

Haydn, Josef. "Allegretto" (from the Military Symphony, 1793). Northport, NY: Arcadian Press, 1993. SATB. This movement can provide a lot of musical interest for a recorder ensemble.

Handel, George. "Hallelujah Chorus" (1741). Northport, NY: Arcadian Press, 1993. SATB. A challenging tune that is arranged well for recorder playing.

Native American Music

Burton, Bryan, and Maria Pondish Kreiter. *Voices of the Wind: Native American Flute Songs.* Danbury, CT: World Music Press, 1998. Outstanding work by nationally known scholars of Native American music.

Chazanoff, Daniel. *Native American Music in Seven Volumes for the Flute or Recorder with Drum/Rattle ad. lib.* Brasstown, NC: Susato Press Folk Series Edition, 1993. For recorder and percussion.

Lacapa, Michael. *The Flute Player: An Apache Folktale.* Flagstaff, AZ: Northland Publishing Co., 1990. Retold and illustrated. Calls for students to play an appropriate and individually conceived melody when story dictates their participation.

Improvisation Materials for the Classroom

Abersold, Jamey. *Nothin' but Blues: How to Play Jazz and Improvise.* New Albany, IN: Jamey Abersold Jazz, Inc., 1978. Provides blues progressions in various keys. The play-along CD accompaniment is helpful for developing fluency in playing with a jazz musician group.

Tinter, Jim. *Big Mouth Blues.* Ft. Worth, TX: Rhythm Band Inc., 1995. Five tunes in contrasting styles with opportunity to improvise. Step-by-step tutorials included and license to copy sheet music.

Tinter, Jim. *A Minor Melody.* Written and recorded solo/echo patterns for improvisation, echo playing, and note reading. Medina, OH: Jim Tinter Productions, 1992 (Available from West Music, 1212 Fifth Street, Coralville, IA 52241).

Recorder-Synthesizer Compositions

Muro, Don. *Six for Two.* Easy duets for soprano recorders and tape. Includes CD. Merrick, NY: J. D. Wall Publishing Co., 1993.

Muro, Don. *Eight More "Easy 8" Songs.* "Add-a-note" songs (each song has one additional note added) until seven tones are represented, including the "D" on the fourth line to the "D" below the treble staff. Includes CD. Merrick, NY: J. D. Wall Publishing Co., 1999.

Muro, Don. *Capriol's Caper: Three Dance Tunes from Arbeau's Orchesographie.* SATB or combinations and tape. Merrick, NY: J. D. Wall Publishing Co., 1982.

Muro, Don. *Introducing B–A–G: Six Very Easy Pieces for Soprano Recorder with Accompaniment on CD.* Merrick, NY: J. D. Wall Publishing Co., 1995.

Muro, Don. *Easy Eight: More "Add-a-Note" Pieces for Synthesizer and Beginning Soprano Recorder.* Merrick, NY: J. D. Wall Publishing Co., 1991.

Reading Sessions at Local Recorder Chapters

The American Recorder Society has chapters throughout the fifty states and Canada. Each chapter has its own schedule of meetings and activities, which include read-throughs of recorder music. Information about local chapters, including contact names and phone numbers, is published in *The American Recorder.*

Journals and Magazines

The Recorder Magazine. Magnamusic Distributors, Inc., PO Box 338, 74 Amenia Union Road, Sharon CT 06069. One of the best sources for information on recorders, music reviews, and articles on the recorder and its literature.

The Orff Echo. American Orff-Schulwerk Association, PO Box 391089, Cleveland, Ohio 44139-8089. A good source of information about teaching music utilizing the Orff approach, which includes the recorder as part of the Instrumentarium.

American Recorder. American Recorder Society, PO Box 631, Littleton, CO 80160-0631; 303-347-1120; e-mail: recorder@compuserve.com. Web site: ourworld.compuserve.com/homepages/recorder. Provides information about the chapter activities of the American Recorder Society and includes music reviews of new recorder compositions.

Music Publishers' Names and Addresses

Arcadian Press (Stan Davis), 116 Scudder Place, Northport, NY 11768.

Berandol Music Limited, 11 St. Joseph Street, Toronto, Canada, M4Y 1J8.

G. Schirmer, Inc. and Associated Music Publishers, Inc., 257 Park Ave South, 20th floor, New York, NY 10010.

GIA Publications, Inc., 7404 S. Mason Ave., Chicago, IL 60638.

Jamey Abersold Jazz, Inc., PO Box 1244, New Albany, IN 47151-1244.

Macie Publishing Company, 10 Astro Place, Suite 100, Rockaway, NJ 07866.

Magnamusic Distributors, Inc., PO Box 338, 74 Amenia Union Road, Sharon CT 06069.

Memphis Musicraft, 4096 Blue Cedar Court, Arlington, TN 38002.

Muse Manifest, 1719 Chino, Santa Barbara, CA 93101.

Polyphonic Publications (Kenneth Andresen), PO Box 7, Colebrook, CT 06021.

Sweet Pipes, 6722 Brentwood Stair Road, Fort Worth, TX 76112; 800-446-1067; fax: 800-576-7608; e-mail: SPMUS@aol.com. Web site: www.sweetpipes.com.

Warner Bros. Publications, 15800 N.W. 48th Avenue, Miami, FL 22014.

Web Sites

Bellugi, David. Hear a professional play the recorder. www.dada.it/webbox/bellugi.htm.

Dolmetsch Workshops. Articles on teaching, history, development of new instruments, and omnibus information about the recorder. www.be-blood.demon.co.uk/index.htm.

Lander, Nicholas. The Recorder Home Page. Probably the most complete source extant for information about the recorder. www.iinet.net.au/~nickl/recorder.html.

MIDIs for Kiddies. Songs and activities for the classroom including musical scores and MIDI downloads. www.pconcentric.net/~Gamba/

On-Line Recorder Method

Learn to Play the Recorder—First Things First. An on-line recorder method for both soprano and alto recorders provided by Brian Blood. Realistic, up-to-date method. Can be heard through the free download Scorch Viewer: www.be-blood.demon.co.uk/method.htm.

Video

The History of Wind Instruments. Venice, FL: Capitol Communications, 1962. Section on recorder shows how they are made. terms, signs, and symbols needed for interpreting and understanding musical examples in the text.

Appendix

Fingering Charts

The fingering charts on the next five pages are from the Web site www.be-blood.co.uk/fingers.com, courtesy of Brian Blood and Dolmetsch Musical Instruments.

Figure 1

English recorder fingering chart

First Octave

These are what we call english, baroque or 'standard' fingerings - the fingerings you should try first on any instrument. In some cases small variations may be necessary for better intonation (e.g. the bottom finger of the right hand for 'top C on descant'/'top F on treble' which can be added/removed as the instrument requires). Use the links above to refer to other fingerings.

Legend: ● = hole covered ○ = hole uncovered ◐ = pinched thumbhole

Recorder: Descant / Tenor / Great Bass	Recorder: Sopranino / Treble / Bass	Thumb	1	2	3	4	5	6a / 6b	7a / 7b	Bell
		-----left hand------				-----right hand-----				
C	F	●	●	●	●	●	●	● / ●	● / ●	
C#/D*b*	F#/G*b*	●	●	●	●	●	●	● / ●	○ / ●	
D	G	●	●	●	●	●	●	● / ●	○ / ○	
D#/E*b*	G#/A*b*	●	●	●	●	●	●	○ / ●	○ / ○	
E	A	●	●	●	●	●	●	○ / ○	○ / ○	
F	A#/B*b*	●	●	●	●	●	○	● / ●	● / ●	
F#/G*b*	B	●	●	●	●	○	●	● / ●	○ / ○	
G	C	●	●	●	●	○	○	○ / ○	○ / ○	
G#/A*b*	C#/D*b*	●	●	●	○	●	●	○ / ●	○ / ○	
A	D	●	●	●	○	○	○	○ / ○	○ / ○	
A#/B*b*	D#/E*b*	●	●	○	●	●	○	○ / ○	○ / ○	
B	E	●	●	○	○	○	○	○ / ○	○ / ○	
		●	○	●	●	○	○	○ / ○	○ / ○	

Figure 2

English recorder fingering chart

Second Octave

These are what we call english, baroque or 'standard' fingerings - the fingerings you should try first on any instrument. In some cases small variations may be necessary for better intonation (e.g. the bottom finger of the right hand for 'top C on descant'/'top F on treble' which can be added/removed as the instrument requires). Use the links above to refer to other fingerings.

Legend: ● = hole covered   ○ = hole uncovered   ◐ = pinched thumbhole

Recorder		Thumb	1	2	3	4	5	6a 6b	7a 7b	Bell
Descant Tenor Great Bass	Sopranino Treble Bass	-----left hand------				-----right hand-----				
C	F	●	○	●	○	○	○	○○	○○	
C#/D*b*	F#/G*b*	○	●	●	○	○	○	○○	○○	
D	G	○	○	●	○	○	○	○○	○○	
		○	●	●	●	●	●	●●	●●	
D#/E*b*	G#/A*b*	○	○	●	●	●	●	●●	○○	
E	A	◐	●	●	●	●	●	○○	○○	
F	A#/B*b*	◐	●	●	●	●	○	●●	○○	
F#/G*b*	B	◐	●	●	●	○	●	○○	○○	
G	C	◐	●	●	●	○	○	○○	○○	
G#/A*b*	C#/D*b*	◐	●	●	○	●	○	○○	○○	
A	D	◐	●	●	○	○	○	○○	○○	
A#/B*b*	D#/E*b*	◐	●	●	○	○	●	●●	○○	
B	E	◐	●	●	○	●	●	○○	○○	

Figure 3

English recorder fingering chart

Third Octave

These are what we call english, baroque or 'standard' fingerings - the fingerings you should try first on any instrument. In some cases small variations may be necessary for better intonation (e.g. the bottom finger of the right hand for 'top C on descant'/'top F on treble' which can be added/removed as the instrument requires). Use the links above to refer to other fingerings.

Legend: ● = hole covered ○ = hole uncovered ◐ = pinched thumbhole

Recorder		Thumb	1	2	3	4	5	6a 6b	7a 7b	Bell
Descant Tenor Great Bass	Sopranino Treble Bass	-----left hand------				-----right hand-----				
C	F	◐	●	○	○	●	●	○○	○○	
C#/D*b*	F#/G*b*	◐	●	○	●	●	○	●●	○○	Close
	G	◐	●	○	●	●	○	●●	○○	
D		◐	●	○	●	●	○	●●	●●	
D#/E*b*	G#/A*b*	◐	○	●	●	○	●	●●	○○	
E	A	◐	○	●	●	○	●	●●	○○	Close
F	A#/B*b*	◐	●	●	○	●	●	○○	○○	Close
F#/G*b*	B	◐	○	●	○	●	●	○○	○○	
G	C	◐	●	○	○	●	○	○○	○○	

Figure 4

English recorder trill fingering chart

First Octave

Legend:		
● = hole covered	○ = hole uncovered	◐ = pinched thumbhole
CO = hole covered then remains open		T = trilling finger

Recorder: Descant, Tenor, Great Bass	Sopranino, Treble, Bass	Thumb (left hand)	1 (left hand)	2 (left hand)	3 (left hand)	4 (right hand)	5 (right hand)	6a/6b (right hand)	7a/7b (right hand)	Bell
D to C	G to F	●	●	●	●	●	●	● ●	T T	
D to C#	G to F#	●	●	●	●	●	●	● ●	○ T	
E to D	A to G	●	●	●	●	●	●	T T	○ ○	
E to D#	A to G#	●	●	●	●	●	●	○ T	○ ○	
F to E	A# to A	●	●	●	●	●	T	CO CO	CO CO	
F# to E	B to A	●	●	●	●	T	●	CO CO	○ ○	
G to F	C to A#	●	●	●	●	T	○	T T	T T	
G to F#	C to B	●	●	●	●	○	T	T T	○ ○	
G# to F#	C# to B	●	●	●	T	CO	●	● ●	○ ○	
G# to G	C# to C	●	●	●	○	T	●	● ●	● ●	
A to G	D to C	●	●	●	T	○	○	○ ○	○ ○	
A to G#	D to C#	●	●	●	○	T	T	○ T	○ ○	
A# to G#	D# to C#	●	●	○	●	T	●	● ●	○ ●	
A# to A	D# to D	●	●	○	●	T	●	○ ●	○ ○	
B to A	E to D	●	●	T	○	○	○	○ ○	○ ○	
B to A#	E to D#	●	●	○	T	●	○	○ ○	○ ○	
C to A#	F to D#	●	T	○	●	●	○	○ ○	○ ○	
C to B	F to E	●	○	●	T	○	○	○ ○	○ ○	
C# to B	F# to E	●	T	○	○	○	○	○ ○	○ ○	

Figure 5

English recorder trill fingering chart

Second Octave

Legend:		
● = hole covered	○ = hole uncovered	◑ = pinched thumbhole
CO = hole covered then remains open		T = trilling finger

Recorder Descant Tenor Great Bass	 Sopranino Treble Bass	Thumb -----left hand------	1	2	3	4 -----right hand-----	5	6a 6b	7a 7b	Bell
C# to C	F# to F	○	●	●	T	○	○	○ ○	○ ○	
D to C	G to F	T	○	●	○	○	○	○ ○	○ ○	
D to C#	G to F#	○	T	●	○	○	○	○ ○	○ ○	
D# to C#	G# to F#	○	T	T	○	○	○	○ ○	○ ○	
D# to D	G# to G	○	●	●	●	T	●	● ●	○ ●	
E to D	A to G	○	●	●	●	●	T	● ●	● ●	
E to D#	A to G#	○	●	●	●	●	●	T T	○ ○	
F to D#	A# to G#	○	●	●	●	●	T	● ●	○ ○	
F to E	A# to A	◑	●	●	●	●	T	CO CO	○ ○	
F# to E	B to A	◑	●	●	●	T	●	○ ○	○ ○	
F# to F	B to A#	◑	●	●	●	○	●	○ T	○ ○	
G to F	C to A#	◑	●	●	●	T	○	T T	○ ○	
G to F#	C to B	◑	●	●	●	○	T	○ ○	○ ○	
G# to F#	C# to B	◑	●	●	○	●	T	○ ○	○ ○	
G# to G	C# to C	◑	●	●	○	●	○	T T	○ ○	
A to G	D to C	◑	●	●	T	○	○	○ ○	○ ○	
A or G#	D or C#	◑	●	●	○	T	○	○ ○	○ ○	
A# to A	D # to D	◑	●	●	T	○	●	● ●	○ ●	
B to A	E to D	CO	●	●	◑	●	●	T T	T T	
B to A#	E to D#	◑	●	●	○	●	●	T T	○ ○	
C to B	F to E	◑	●	T	○	●	●	○ ○	○ ○